And What Marvel!

By
Dr. Gary L. Mann

© Dr. Gary L. Mann
October 2020

6178 Lakewood Drive
Gilmer, Texas 75645
Dr.gmann75@gmail.com

ISBN: 978-1-7356723-3-5

All Scripture references are from the King James Bible

All Rights Reserved
No part of this book may be reproduced in any form without permission in writing from the author or publisher, except for the inclusion of brief quotations in a review.

Many of the quotes are copied and pasted exactly as they were in my computer with proper reference on who I took the quote from. Their quotes are helpful in these areas but my quoting men does not mean I agree with all their theology and every thing they say.

Formatting and Publishing assisted by
The Old Paths Publications, Inc.
Cleveland, GA 30528
Web address: www.theoldpathspublications.com
Email: TOP@theoldpathspublications.com
Office Phones: 706-865-0153 or 706-219-2153
Cell Phone: 706-461-1611

THE COVER

The cover for this material has special meaning. The blank paper represents the originals before God breathed to the human author the words of the Word of God. The Greek and the Hebrew open books represent the Hebrew Masoretic text and the Textus Receptus. They were the original languages God gave the Scriptures in. The Bible on top of the Hebrew and Greek books is the King James Bible which is based on the texts under it. This shows the process of Inspiration, Preservation and Translation.

DEDICATION

"To all the faithful men in the past who revered the Word of God and who not only passed it down to succeeding generations but who also hazarded their lives and their possessions to pass down to us the same things it taught them."

Dr. Gary L. Mann
October 2020

RECOMMENDATIONS

And What Marvel! by Dr. Gary L. Mann is a valuable source for anyone who is interested in separating fact from fiction concerning the King James Bible. His book will assist you in getting "up to speed" concerning the many points of controversy that are associated with the King James Bible. Dr. Mann gives thorough treatment showing facts and flaws of the different views of Inspiration, Preservation and Translation. You will find his book a valuable and understandable book that is worth reading and recommending to others.

David L. Brown, Ph.D., President,
King James Bible Research Council
2020

"Dr. Gary L. Mann has performed a great service to all of us by authoring this volume. There are so many thoughts by many individuals today concerning "inspiration," "preservation," and "translation" that do not line up with Scripture. Obviously, Dr. Mann has spent many hours studying, praying, reflecting, and researching on these issues, but the **foundation** he uses is the Words of God, not what man "thinks" or has "written." Every pastor, evangelist, missionary, and man in the pew would do well to take time to study this volume. We pray it will have wide circulation among those who are confused or need a refreshing about these doctrinal issues. We highly recommend it."

H. D. Williams, M.D., Ph.D.,
President
The Old Paths Publications
October 2020

TABLE OF CONTENTS

Contents
DEDICATION **3**
RECOMMENDATIONS **4**
TABLE OF CONTENTS **5**
AND WHAT MARVEL! **7**
SECTION 1 .... **8**
Introduction **8**
Statement #1 .... **9**
  Preface 9
Statement #2 .... **10**
  Introduction 10
Statement #3 .... **14**
  Bible Doctrinal Statement 14
Chapter 1 .... **16**
  The Same Thing! 16
Chapter 2 .... **22**
  God's Word! 22
Section 2 .... **29**
  Salvation 29
Chapter 3 .... **30**
  The Real Importance of Scripture 30
Chapter 4 .... **31**
  What is Necessary to Understand Scripture? 31
Section 3 .... **39**
  Inspiration 39
Chapter 5 .... **40**
  The Case for "God-Breathed!" 40
    Verses to Consider 53
Chapter 6 .... **56**
  The Holy Spirit and God's Word 56
Chapter 7 .... **68**
  The Efficacy of the Scriptures 68
Chapter 8 .... **87**
  Preserved and Continuous Inspiration? 87
    EXPLANATORY NOTES AND QUAINT SAYINGS. 97
    EXPLANATORY NOTES AND QUAINT SAYINGS. 101
Chapter 9 .... **113**
  Willingly Ignorant? 113

Chapter 10 .... **122**
  What About Dual and Triple Inspiration? 122
Section 4 .... **136**
  Preservation 136
Chapter 11 .... **137**
  Preservation 137
Chapter 12 .... **147**
  Preservation, An Important Part of the Process 147
Chapter 13 .... **162**
  Preservation, the Crux of the Matter 162
Chapter 14 .... **168**
  Antioch and Alexandria 168
Chapter 15 .... **182**
  Heretical Teachings About Preservation 182
Section 5 .... **189**
  Translation 189
Chapter 16 .... **190**
  Why We Needed a Translation 190
Chapter 17 .... **198**
  The Translators' Companies and Their Guidelines 198
Chapter 18 .... **202**
  Dynamic and Formal Equivalence 202
Chapter 19 .... **210**
  The Translators 210
Chapter 20 .... **216**
  More Reasons the Men of Hampton Court Were Not Inspired
  216
ABOUT THE AUTHOR **233**

AND WHAT MARVEL!

This is a part of the preface, which was written by the translators, who I call the "Men of Hampton Court" of the Authorized Version (King James Bible) and appeared in the original 1611 printing.

"And what marvel? the original being from heaven, not from earth; the author being God, not man; the inditer, the Holy Spirit, not the wit of the Apostles or Prophets; the penmen, such as were sanctified from the womb, and endued with a principal portion of God's Spirit; the matter, verity, piety, purity, uprightness; the form, God's word, God's testimony, God's oracles, the word of truth, the word of salvation; the effects, light of understanding, stableness of persuasion, repentance from dead works, newness of life, holiness, peace, joy in the Holy Ghost; lastly the end and reward of the study thereof, fellowship with the saints, participation of the heavenly nature, fruition of an inheritance immortal, undefiled, and that never shall fade away; Happy is the man that delighteth in the Scripture, and thrice happy that meditateth in it day and night."

SECTION 1
Introduction

Statement #1

Preface

How did we get God's Word? Do we have God's Word? Where can I find God's Word? Is the Bible written by God or men? How did we end up with the King James Bible and all the versions? These and many, many more questions will be answered in this book, and, hopefully, by the end of it you will have a much better understanding of the Bible and the answers to these questions.

In November of 2014 I was asked to teach things about the Bible to a church with a boarding school for boys. I knew I had to keep it simple and all the information very basic and keep it interesting. I also had the challenge of keeping it interesting enough for the adults who were there. What a challenge! Much of this material comes from that and my study of the many topics in connection with the Bible.

Since then, I have added much helpful and a little bit deeper material to get a complete grasp of the situation and help settle in the minds of the readers that the Kings James Bible is what we should continue to use and that it is THE Word of God for the English speaking people,. I trust that your study of the Bible will increase and that your life will continue to be richly blessed by the reading and study of the Word of God.

Statement #2

Introduction

There is a very interesting verse found in John 21:25 which says, "And there are also many other things which Jesus did, the which, if they should be written every one, I suppose that even the world itself could not contain the books that should be written. Amen." This verse recently has been taught that there is more of the Word of God in heaven and that God only gave us the parts of it that He thought we needed in the 66 books of the canon of Scripture. This verse is NOT teaching that. As a matter of fact if you look back to John 20:30 it says, "And many other signs truly did Jesus in the presence of his disciples, which are not written in this book:" Connecting these two verses together we see that it is teaching that if all the things Jesus had done while He was on the earth had been written down in the Bible, the world could not contain the books that should be written. There would be a huge Bible then and there would be an innumerable amount of books also that would be written by human authors about all that information.

This leads me to a question and my answer. Thinking about the myriads of books in existence, and more being added all the time concerning the Bible, why another book on how we ended up with the King James Bible? I can hear the question being asked, "Aren't there enough books already written on this subject?" My answer is, yes, and no!

Yes, there are plenty of books already in print on this process, but no, there are still good reasons for another such book to be written.

First of all, many, if not most, of the books on this subject have been written from an *"Alexandrian"* view point and not on an *"Antioch"* one. I will not take a lot of time and space in this introduction to explain that but will simply say that I believe

INTRODUCTION

there is a HUGE need for material to be written, not from an Alexandrian, or New Evangelical, point of view, but from the Antioch or Biblical point of view. We do not need any more material from the Critical Text (Alexandrian) crowd, but from a Biblical, or Received Text (Antioch) crowd. Because of a huge neglect of writing from a Biblical viewpoint (Antioch), we have been inundated with non-Biblical (Alexandrian) material, and this must be stopped!

As you read and study the information in this book, you will understand more completely what I mean concerning the differences between the Alexandrian and Antioch teachings and will understand then the true process of how we ended up with the King James Bible and why we say that it is the Bible the English speaking people should use and not the Alexandrian versions.

Another reason this book and other material like it should be written is because Biblical Christianity has for far too long allowed the New Evangelicals and others to control the conversation through their constant flooding of the book market leaving Biblical Christianity with nothing to read from a historical and Biblical perspective. Therefore, Biblical Christianity does not have an understanding of many topics including the process of Inspiration, Preservation and Translation of the Word of God. Our graduates are leaving college without the basic understanding of this process let alone the difference between the Alexandrian and Antioch mindset and are therefore beginning to use the Alexandrian versions like the English Standard Version and others. This too must be stopped!

Lastly, this material is needed because of the amount of false teaching that is happening among Biblical Christianity in their effort to "fill the gap," so to speak having especially to do with understanding the process of Biblical inspiration, preservation and translation of Scriptures. Without knowing it the teaching I am hearing and seeing is a blend of Alexandrian and

Antioch teachings but as the Scripture so plainly warns, **"A little leaven leaveneth the whole lump."** (Galatians 5:8)

Titus, by revelation, was dealing with false teaching by false teachers. Titus 1:10 and 11 states, "For there are many unruly and vain talkers and deceivers, specially they of the circumcision: Whose mouths must be stopped, who subvert whole houses, teaching things which they ought not, for filthy lucre's sake." Then we have Titus 2:1 which gives us a mandate when it says, "But speak thou the things which become sound doctrine" He then gave a list of the sound doctrine he was expressing the need to be taught in the following verses, which have nothing to do with my topic but the principle is the same.

In writing about Titus 2:1 John Gill wrote,

"But speak thou the things which become sound doctrine. The things which become it are a good life and conversation, the various duties incumbent on professors of religion, according to their different station, age, and sex, which are observed in some following verses; these become the Gospel of Christ, and are ornamental to the doctrine of God our Saviour; and <u>these are to be spoken of by the ministers of Christ, in their proper places, and at proper times; who ought not to be dumb, and keep silence at any time, but especially when there are many unruly and vain talkers: sound doctrine ought to be spoken out openly and publicly, fully and faithfully, with great plainness and evidence, that it may be understood and known by all; and with much certainty, without hesitation, as being, without controversy, undoubted truth; and with all boldness, not fearing men, or seeking to please them; and it should be constantly and continually spoken, in season, and out of season; and care should be taken that it be spoken consistently, and</u>

INTRODUCTION

<u>in an uniform manner, that there be no clashing and contradiction;</u> and the duties of religion, which become sound doctrine, should be set in their true light, and proper place, as fruits of the grace of God, and to glorify him; these should be spoken out plainly, frequently insisted upon, and warmly and zealously urged, as being decent things, for the honor of God, the recommending of religion, the good of mankind, and the service of one another:"

With the large amount of Alexandrian teaching and material, and the lack of Antioch material and teaching we then have a weak understanding and outright false teaching that is taking place among Bible Christianity on the process of inspiration, preservation and translation of the Bible. There is a need for this material and more. It is not all that needs to be written and taught, but I do pray that this material will be read, understood, taught and will cause Bible believing Christians everywhere to get involved in adding more Biblical material. This is a part of discipleship and the propagation of the Bible…sound doctrine! To neglect publishing books with sound doctrine is to allow Satan to teach false doctrine and cause more confusion. We have taken the back seat for far too long with our anti-book, anti-writing and fear of writing attitude and we must step up to the plate and write and publish doctrinal material that will counter the Alexandrian mind-set and bring out the Antioch one. May it be so.

Dr. Gary L. Mann

Statement #3

Bible Doctrinal Statement

I believe the Holy Bible was written by men supernaturally "moved;" that it has truth for its matter without any admixture of error; that it is and shall remain to the end of the age the only complete and final revelation of the will of God to man; and that it is the true center of Christian union and the supreme standard by which all human conduct, creeds, and opinions should be tried.

- I believe the Authorized (King James) Bible, Old and New Testaments, is the Word of God kept intact for English-speaking peoples by way of God's divine providence and work of preservation; and that the Authorized Version translators were not "inspired." but were merely God's instruments used to preserve His words for English-speaking peoples.
- By Holy Bible I mean that collection of sixty-six books, from Genesis to Revelation, which, as originally written and providentially preserved, does not only contain and convey the Word of God, but is the very Word of God.
- By inspiration I mean that the books of the Bible were written by holy men of God as they were moved by the Holy Ghost in such a definite way that their writings were supernaturally and verbally inspired and free from error, as no other writings have ever been or ever will be inspired.
- By providentially preserved I mean that God through the ages has, in His divine providence, preserved the very words that He inspired; that the Hebrew Old Testament text, as found in the traditional Masoretic text, and the Greek New Testament text, as found in the Textus Receptus, are indeed the products of God's providential

preservation and are altogether the complete, preserved, inerrant word of God.

Chapter 1

The Same Thing!

2 Timothy 2:2

> *"And the things that thou hast heard of me among many witnesses, the same commit thou to faithful men, who shall be able to teach others also."*

While preaching recently in a friend's church in Florida, I noticed that on both sides of the auditorium hanging on the walls were many portraits of preachers of the past. The portraits were drawings of men like John R. Rice, Tom Malone, Bill Rice, J. Frank Norris, Charles Spurgeon, Lee Roberson, R.G. Lee and many others. I was preaching from 2 Timothy 1:1-19 on faithfulness where Paul told Timothy some key things about being faithful, especially in verse 13 which states, **"Hold fast the form of sound words, which thou hast heard of me, in faith and love which is in Christ Jesus."** This began a theme in 2 Timothy which is picked up again in 2 Timothy 2:2 which says, **"And the things that thou hast heard of me among many witnesses, the same commit thou to faithful men, who shall be able to teach others also."**

If you will notice there are 4 generations of people mentioned in this verse. Paul is speaking to Timothy who is told to teach the same thing to another generation of faithful men who then is responsible to teach the same things to another generation of people. This shows us the importance of teaching the same things to people, or, being faithful to teach the same things that are Biblical to the next generation.

Another important and familiar verse in 2 Timothy is found in chapter 2 verse 15 which says, **"Study to shew thyself approved unto God, a workman that needeth not to be ashamed, rightly dividing the word of truth."** I have often taught about this verse that if study causes us to rightly divide the

CHAPTER 1: THE SAME THING!

word of truth then a lack of study causes us to wrongly divide it. Again, there is the theme of faithfulness.

Then in chapter 2 verse 24 is the following, **"And the servant of the Lord must not strive; but be gentle unto all men, apt to teach, patient,"** The emphasis here that I want to point out is that the preacher is supposed to be "apt (have the ability), to teach." Teach what? The same things of course.

Finally in 2 Timothy 3:14-17 Paul wrote, "But continue thou in the things which thou hast learned and hast been assured of, knowing of whom thou hast learned *them;* And that from a child thou hast known the holy scriptures, which are able to make thee wise unto salvation through faith which is in Christ Jesus. All scripture *is* given by inspiration of God, and *is* profitable for doctrine, for reproof, for correction, for instruction in righteousness: That the man of God may be perfect, throughly furnished unto all good works." In this section we see that Paul told Timothy to, "…continue thou in the things which thou hast learned…" So whatever he had learned, he was to continue in them; he was to put them in practice in his life. We also see the main source of the material that he learned from and that of course is what the Scriptures say. So, He had learned the Scripture from teachers, he was to continue in them and he was to teach the same things to faithful men who would then teach the same things to others.

The criticism by some on this material is going to be the use of quotes from an older generation. Some of the criticisms will come from men who, simply put, don't like some of the men that will be quoted. But, the "men on the wall," are the ones who were taught by their predecessors and then they taught the same things to us on inspiration, preservation and translation. Their "Paul" had taught them that inspiration means "God breathed," and that is what the "men on the wall" taught us. Their "Paul" taught them that God had promised to preserve His Word to all generations. Their "Paul" taught them that the King James Bible was an accurate and faithful translation, and they then taught faithful men the same things who are supposed to pass down to the next generation those same Biblical truths.

The teachings we received from our "Paul's" on inspiration, preservation and translation are historically and Biblically accurate. Verbal inspiration is still true today. The teaching that God breathed the words of the Word of God is still accurate today. God gave us Scripture by inspiration! Inspiration is not what God did TO the Scripture; it is how God GAVE us the Scriptures in the Old and New Testaments.

A few today have **changed** what they have been taught. Some have done this to distance themselves from individuals they do not like. The problem with some change is that the ones who change what the Scriptures teach sometimes go too far the other way from the ones that they try to distance themselves from then coming up with their own false teachings.

Through all these changes I have been very slow and deliberate in my study and research for this material (taking well over 5 years to look at it all), and have determined that our "Paul's" were not wrong. They were taught the same things they taught us and we are not to change those teachings.

I also see the scholarship of the men on the wall as compared to those today, and can readily see that there is no comparison. While the men of today who have changed what they used to teach, even sometimes basing their teaching on a woman's material, go around pounding themselves on their chest and telling us the men on the wall were wrong and even deceived, I see the men on the walls abilities compared to those of today and cringe at the huge disparity. The men on the wall were true students of Scripture, history, accurate Bible study and even Greek and Hebrew. While the men who were supposed to teach the same things don't even know the Greek alphabet and refuse to use materials that were designed to help us in our Bible study and even come up with weird definitions based on poor Bible study methods.

CHAPTER 1: THE SAME THING!

The men of today make comments like, "There was no perfect Bible until 1611," while the men of yesterday all agreed with God that He would preserve His Word for every generation.

The men of today teach that the English corrects the Greek and Hebrew meaning that the languages God gave us the Word of God in were somehow either wrong or not preserved, while the men of yesteryear not only could quote the Greek and Hebrew from memory but used it consistently in agreement with the English of the King James Bible

The men of today call a person a liberal if they believe the Greek word "THEOPNEUSTOS" means God breathed and teach that it really means that God PUT His breath into the Word of God totally ignoring the Spirit of God's work in conjunction with the Word of God. Inspiration is not what God did to the Scriptures; it is how God gave the Scriptures. They continue their accusations by saying that these liberals were influenced by books that were written by sinful men. Well, what book besides the Bible isn't written by sinful men? What message preached is not preached by sinful men. If we are to ignore the writings of men in their books because they were sinners then I guess we should not listen to messages preached by sinful men! John Gill, who lived in the 1700's, believed THEOPNEUSTOS meant God breathed because of his knowledge of the Greek and Latin. He was not "poisoned" by the Strong's Concordance, because it had not been published yet. Charles Spurgeon had also not been "infested" by a Concordance for the same reason but knew THEOPNEUSTOS meant God breathed. They were not liberals, they had been faithfully taught by their men on the wall and taught the same thing to others who were to teach the same thing to others who would teach us those same things!

Those men on the wall, and hundreds and thousands of others, including the men of Hampton Court (the translators of the King James Bible), understood and taught the process of inspiration, preservation and translation and I for one will continue to teach faithful men what I was taught about it who will then teach others those same things BECAUSE THEY ARE HISTORICALLY AND BIBLICALLY SOUND! You can't get any better than that. The same thing!

The men of Hampton Court also knew the dangers in connection with their work of translation. In their letter to the reader they wrote, "…whosoever attempteth anything for the publick (especially if it pertains to Religion, and to the opening and clearing of the word of God), the same setteth himself upon a stage to be gloated upon by every evil eye, yea, he casteth himself headlong upon pikes, to be gored by every sharp tongue. For he that meddleth with man's religion in any part, meddleth with their custom, nay, with their freehold; and though they find no content in that which they have, yet they cannot abide to hear of altering." They were well aware, as was King James that the detractors would come and gnash on them with their teeth!

I too fully expect those who I often refer to as those who have, "drank the Kool-Aid," to reveal their venom with accusations and ridicule. I get that. Never-the-less, I felt it necessary to once again teach "What thus saith the Lord," on these subjects and quote from the men of Hampton Court and others as much as possible so we can once again reclaim the tried and true Biblical and historical teachings on the process of inspiration, preservation and translation.

I have spent too many years in this study and refuse to agree with the NEW teaching; and I have read, listened to and studied these NEW teachings and even had some conversations with some about these NEW teachings.

I firmly remain on the side of the great preachers of the past from my studies of their writings and messages as far back as the late 1600's until now. I firmly remain with Biblical studies not only on my own but from those who in the past accomplished great things for God as compared to the detractors and their NEW teachings who have lost marriages, churches and their buildings

CHAPTER 1: THE SAME THING!

and who have changed in their doctrine because of an agenda or personality clashes and jealousy.

I firmly remain with those in the past who knew the languages, who could read and write them fluently compared to those today who barely know their own language and who even refuse to refer to a dictionary in their own language. Here-in I stand, and I stand with the same things as they were taught to me from those in the past and many in the present, because they are Biblically and historically correct.

Chapter 2

God's Word!

In their letter to the readers the men of Hampton Court wrote, "And this is the **Word of God,** which we translate." The Word of God or God's Word. It is called, "God's Word!" The Bible is called that because it is **God's** Word or words. It is God's words, not men's word. **2 Peter 1:20 &21 "Knowing this first, that no prophecy of the scripture is of any private interpretation. For the prophecy came not in old time by the will of man: but holy men of God spake** *as they were* **moved by the Holy Ghost."** Again in their letter to the readers the men of Hampton Court wrote in reference to God's Word, "…the Author being God, not man; the inditer the Holy Spirit, not the wit of the apostles or prophets…" This is God's Word, not man's!

In 2 Samuel 23:1 & 2, we see some of David's last words speaking about God's word. He said, "Now these *be* the last words of David. David the son of Jesse said, and the man *who was* raised up on high, the anointed of the God of Jacob, and the sweet psalmist of Israel, said, The Spirit of the LORD spake by me, and his word *was* in my tongue." In his very helpful work on God's Word, John Gill wrote about this verse,

"The Spirit of the Lord spake by me,…. The psalms and songs he composed were not the fruits of his own genius, but were written by him under the inspiration of the Spirit of God; by whom holy men of God, the penmen of the Scriptures, spoke, even as they were moved by the Holy Ghost, of whom David was one, being a prophet; see **Act 1:16 Act 2:30**; so the Targum here, "David spoke by the spirit of prophecy of the Lord:' 'or spake "in me"; what he spoke was first internally impressed upon his mind by the Spirit of God, and then he expressed it with his tongue, as follows: **and his word** *was* **in my tongue**; not only the matter of his psalms was indited by the Spirit of God, and

CHAPTER 2: GOD'S WORD!

suggested to his mind; but the very words in which they are delivered were given to him, and he was directed to make use of them, and did." It is clear what David wrote were God's words, not his own. **This is the process of inspiration**.

A very familiar set of verses which will be referred to often is found in 2 Peter 1:16-21 which states, "For we have not followed cunningly devised fables, when we made known unto you the power and coming of our Lord Jesus Christ, but were eyewitnesses of his majesty. For he received from God the Father honour and glory, when there came such a voice to him from the excellent glory, This is my beloved Son, in whom I am well pleased. And this voice which came from heaven we heard, when we were with him in the holy mount. We have also a more sure word of prophecy; whereunto ye do well that ye take heed, as unto a light that shineth in a dark place, until the day dawn, and the day star arise in your hearts: Knowing this first, that no prophecy of the scripture is of any private interpretation. <u>For the prophecy came not in old time by the will of man: but holy men of God spake *as they were* moved by the Holy Ghost.</u>" Again, Gill wrote the following on verse 21,

> ***2 Peter 1:21*** *For the prophecy came not in old time by the will of man: but holy men of God spake as they were moved by the Holy Ghost.*
>
> **"For the prophecy**,.... The whole Scripture, all the prophetic writings; so the Jews call the Scriptures הנבואה, "the prophecy" (g), by way of eminence, and from the subject matter of the sacred word:
>
> **came not in old time by the will of man**; was not brought into the world at first, or in any period of time, as and when man would, according to his pleasure, and as he thought fit: neither Moses, nor David, nor Isaiah, nor Jeremiah, nor Ezekiel, nor Daniel, nor any other of the prophets, prophesied

when they pleased, but when it was the will of God they should; they were stirred up to prophesy, not by any human impulse, but by a divine influence:

but holy men of God; such as he sanctified by his Spirit, and separated from the rest of men to such peculiar service; and whom he employed as public ministers of his word: for so this phrase "men", or "man of God", often signifies, 1Sa 2:27.

spake, as they were moved by the Holy Ghost; who illuminated their minds, gave them a knowledge of divine things, and a foresight of future ones; dictated to them what they should say or write; and moved upon them strongly, and by a secret and powerful impulse stirred them up to deliver what they did, in the name and fear of God: **which shows the authority of the Scriptures, that they are the word of God, and not of men;** and as such should be attended to, and received with all affection and reverence; and that the Spirit is the best interpreter of them, who first dictated them; and that they are to be the rule of our faith and practice; nor are we to expect any other, until the second coming of Christ."

This is God's word, not David's, not Moses, not John's words, they are God's Words not man's! This is why we call the Bible God's Word! We see, "Thus saith the Lord" in 413 verses throughout the Bible and then what God said. This is God's Word!

In order for the Bible to become effective at all, you must first of all accept what is written as God's Word, not mans. If it is God's Word then it has all the authority behind it. If it is man's word then there is no authority and only a man's opinion.

CHAPTER 2: GOD'S WORD!

In reading John R. Rice's book entitled <u>Our God-Breathed Book – The Bible,</u> I found something interesting and wrote a note in the pages of it saying, "Do not approach a study of the Bible to SEE if it is God's Word; but study it AS God's Word." On the next page Dr. Rice wrote,

> "We come bowing to its authority as the authority of God and of Christ. We come to believe all its statements, to humbly try to follow its commandments, to claim gladly as many of its promises as our frail faith can claim."

How can we do that? By understanding it IS God's Word, not man's word! Thus, when it says in 2 Timothy 3:16 that, "All scripture *is* given by inspiration of God, and *is* profitable for doctrine, for reproof, for correction, for instruction in righteousness:" that is exactly what it means! This is God's Word and must be approached as such. It must be studied as God's Word! It must be yielded to as God's Word. It is not just a book ABOUT God, it is His Word and we are commanded to study it AS His Word! We must stand firmly upon the fact that the Bible, the King James Bible in the English language, is God's Word!

As God's Word, we are not to tamper with it or change it in any way. Those of the Alexandrian line have changed God's Word to make it theirs, not God's. They still do not believe we have all of it, because, they think, we might find more if it somewhere. They did not believe in the inspiration of Scripture and are now of the mindset that we cannot know what God has said, thus, a new "Bible for every generation, gender, and gnostic."

As God's Word we are to protect it and stand for it let come what may. We are to earnestly contend for the faith and not allow it to be damaged in any way. It is God's Word!

In the Garden of Eden God communed with Adam and Eve. God spoke with them in their language and we have some of that conversation in our Bible. Go has always communicated with mankind. How? By using WORDS! The same is true with the Bible and how He gave it to us. He did not just breath on the words; He breathed, or spoke, the words of the Word of God. THAT is what inspiration is! As I will say elsewhere in this book, Inspiration is not what God did TO the Bible; inspiration is how God GAVE the Bible! God uses words to communicate with man. This is God's Word and the very fact that it is God's Word and that He always communicated with mankind using words is why it is called God's Word!

Now notice some other rather revealing facts about God's Word. God's Word came from the mouth of God! Isn't that deep! In Revelation 1:16 it says, **"And he had in his right hand seven stars: <u>and out of his mouth went a sharp twoedged sword</u>: and his countenance** *was* **as the sun shineth in his strength."** Notice carefully that it says, **"...and out of his mouth went a sharp twoedged sword..."** What is this sharp twoedged sword? We get another glimpse of this in Hebrews 4:12 where it states, **"For the word of God** *is* **quick, and powerful, and <u>sharper than any twoedged sword</u>, piercing even to the dividing asunder of soul and spirit, and of the joints and marrow, and** *is* **a discerner of the thoughts and intents of the heart."** (There are some who teach that the Bible actually THINKS using this verse as their proof, but I will get back to that in another chapter.) Notice the phrase, **"...sharper than any twoedged sword..."** There is that same phrase as used in Revelation where the sharp two edged sword comes out of the mouth of God. This phrase comes after the description in Hebrews 4:12 telling us what this sharp two edged sword is, "For the word of God..." The words of God are sharper than any two edged sword. God's Word is sharp! God's Word is called the two edged sword! Where does this sword proceed from? **FROM HIS MOUTH!** It is God's Word, or, what God says, that is sharper than any two edged sword!

In **Ephesians 6:17** we see this, **"And take the helmet of salvation, <u>and the sword of the Spirit, which is the word of God</u>:"** The sword of the Spirit, or what the Spirit uses, is the

CHAPTER 2: GOD'S WORD!

Word of God. The Word of God is the sword of the Spirit. Isn't it great that in the English word sword used here is also the word, "word?" I love the "coincidences" of the Bible in the English language. Again, a reference in the Scriptures that what God has said is a sword and that sword comes out of His mouth. It is God's Word, or, God's communications with man, it is God's breathed, or spoken Word!

Notice in Matthew 4:4 (which quotes a part of Deuteronomy 8:3), it says, "But he answered and said, It is written, Man shall not live by bread alone, <u>but by every word that proceedeth out of the mouth of God."</u> This again tells us where we got God's Word. It comes from and is the Sword of the Spirit which is sharper than any two edged sword and it comes from the mouth of God! The Bible is God's Word!

To me a hugely interesting verse which shows us how God created the world is found in **Psalm 33:6** which says, **"By the <u>word of the Lord</u> were the heavens made; and all the host of them <u>BY THE BREATH OF HIS MOUTH!"</u>** In this case God breathed and spoke and there was light. He created the heavens and the earth by speaking! He gave us the Word of God by speaking! In the creation of the world in Genesis 1:3 it says, **"And God said…"** Before He created, He spoke! He spoke the world into existence and God's Word always came from the mouth of God! **THIS is why it is called God's Word or the Word of God!**

The phrase, "the Word of the Lord" is found 264 times in 261 verses. "Thus saith the Lord" is in 413 verses in Scripture. "The word of the Lord came…in a vision" is found 9 times in 8 verses. "Thus shalt thou say" is found in 10 verses and the phrase "say unto them" is in 75 verses used 76 times. The phrase "His word was in my mouth" is found in Numbers 22:38 and 23:12. "Out of His mouth" is in Proverbs 2:6; Revelation 1:16; 19:15 and verse 21.

God's Word proceeds out of His mouth! It is God's Word; it is how He communicated with mankind and how He gave us all Scripture! The process of inspiration is Him breathing, or speaking the very words to holy men of old. All Scripture is GIVEN by inspiration. **IT IS GOD'S WORD!**

Section 2
Salvation

Chapter 3

The Real Importance of Scripture

From the letter to the readers the men of Hampton Court (the translators) had this to say, "...blessed be they, and most hounoured be their name, that break the ice, (by translation) and give the onset upon that which helpeth forward to the saving of souls. Now what can be more available thereto, than to deliver God's book unto God's people in a tongue which they understand."

The men of Hampton Court knew that the common people needed the Word of God in their language so it would help forward the saving of souls. There are many reasons why God gave us His Word but the most important one must be for the saving of souls. Without the Scriptures in the vulgar language (the language the people can read and understand) how are they to learn of salvation? How are they to learn of Christ except through the preaching and now in the printed page?

The translators also wrote the following on the importance of the Scripture in the language of the people. "But how shall men meditate in that which they cannot understand? How shall they understand that which is kept close in an unknown tongue?" They went on to write a little later, "It is necessary to have translations in a readiness. Translation it is that openeth the window, to let in the light." They knew their job was very important to the common people who they knew needed a translation so the light of the Gospel should come in to the saving of souls.

In this section on "SALVATION," we will see what is necessary to understand the Scriptures

Chapter 4

What is Necessary to Understand Scripture?

1 Corinthians 2:1-16 says,

> *"And I, brethren, when I came to you, came not with excellency of speech or of wisdom, declaring unto you the testimony of God. For I determined not to know anything among you, save Jesus Christ, and him crucified. And I was with you in weakness, and in fear, and in much trembling. And my speech and my preaching was not with enticing words of man's wisdom, but in demonstration of the Spirit and of power: That your faith should not stand in the wisdom of men, but in the power of God. Howbeit we speak wisdom among them that are perfect: yet not the wisdom of this world, nor of the princes of this world, that come to nought: But we speak the wisdom of God in a mystery, even the hidden wisdom, which God ordained before the world unto our glory: Which none of the princes of this world knew: for had they known it, they would not have crucified the Lord of glory. But as it is written, Eye hath not seen, nor ear heard, neither have entered into the heart of man, the things which God hath prepared for them that love him. But God hath revealed them unto us by his Spirit: for the Spirit searcheth all things, yea, the deep things of God. For what man knoweth the things of a man, save the spirit of man which is in him? even so the things of God knoweth no man, but the Spirit of God. Now we have received, not the spirit of the world, but the spirit which is of*

God; that we might know the things that are freely given to us of God. Which things also we speak, not in the words which man's wisdom teacheth, but which the Holy Ghost teacheth; comparing spiritual things with spiritual. **<u>But the natural man receiveth not the things of the Spirit of God: for they are foolishness unto him: neither can he know *them*, because they are spiritually discerned.</u>** *But he that is spiritual judgeth all things, yet he himself is judged of no man. For who hath known the mind of the Lord, that he may instruct him? But we have the mind of Christ."*

Please notice the emphasized section of this set of verses. It is actually verse 14. It says, "But the natural man receiveth not the things of the Spirit of God: for they are foolishness unto him: neither can he know *them*, because they are spiritually discerned."

One of the common statements made, especially about the King James Bible, is that it is too hard to understand. Yet, according to D.A. Waite in the Defined King James Bible the average King James Bible readability level is grade level 5.63. In other words, a 5th grader can read and understand the King James Bible. The most difficult book in the Bible to read is Jude with a 9.11 grade level and the easiest is the book of Psalms which is a 3.91 grade level ability. So, the Bible is not really all that hard to read or understand. Then, WHAT IS THE REAL PROBLEM? Why, according to many people is the King James Bible "hard" to understand?

The first thing we need to understand is that there is a huge difference between the Bible and other books. The Bible was NOT written by men while all other books have been written by men. In 2 Timothy 3:16 we see, "**All scripture *is* given by inspiration of God**, and *is* profitable for doctrine, for reproof, for correction, for instruction in righteousness:" then in 2 Peter 1:20 and 21 it clearly states, "Knowing this first, that no prophecy of

CHAPTER 4: WHAT IS NECESSARY TO UNDERSTAND SCRIPTURE

the scripture is of any private interpretation. **For the prophecy came not in old time by the will of man: but holy men of God spake *as they were* moved by the Holy Ghost."** No other book in existence has that claim! NONE!

The two major differences as already stated is that the Bible was written by God, not by men and all other books, including this one, is written by men and not God! Now here is a major point in want to insert here and will be mention later. The versions that come from the Alexandrian line of manuscripts have all been tampered with by men. They will even say things like, "the Bible

The Bible was given to man by inspiration, and you will totally understand what that is in the next section, through the Holy Spirit of God. The verse in 1 Corinthians 2 verse 14 again says, **"But the natural man receiveth not the things of the Spirit of God: for they are foolishness unto him: neither can he know *them*, because they are spiritually discerned."** Now let me break down this verse a little.

- But the natural man – the unsaved person
- **receiveth not the things of the Spirit of God** – cannot understand things of or by the Spirit of God
- **for they are foolishness unto him: -** Because the unsaved person cannot understand the thigs of or by the Spirit of God they then seem foolish to them. (1 Corinthians 1:18 **For the preaching of the cross is to them that perish foolishness;** but unto us which are saved it is the power of God.)
- **neither can he know *them* –** the unsaved person CANNOT understand the things of the Spirit of God (WHY?)
- **because they are spiritually discerned. –** The unsaved person CANNOT understand the things of the Spirit of God (the Bible) because it is SPIRITUALLY discerned or given! The Bible is spiritually discerned or given by the Spirit of God. The unsaved person even with

a college degree CANNOT truly understand the Bible and it even looks foolish to them because it is a book given by the Spirit of God!

Let me throw in this test to you right here. The Bible says that the things of the Spirit of God are FOOLISHNESS to the natural (unsaved) man, and the preaching of the Gospel of Christ is FOOLISHNESS to those who perish. Does this describe you? If so, please keep reading this chapter. It can make all the difference in the world and even in eternity.

To go into a little more detail here let me say this, Paul, the man God used to write 1 Corinthians, stated the reason why some have a tough time understanding the Word of God is because they are a NATURAL man. A NATURAL man Biblically, is one who has been born of the flesh (when is your natural birthday?), and not of the Spirit. We see this taught in the Book of John chapter three. In **John 3:1-7** it clearly states,

> *1. There was a man of the Pharisees, named Nicodemus, a ruler of the Jews:*
>
> *2. The same came to Jesus by night, and said unto him, Rabbi, we know that thou art a teacher come from God: for no man can do these miracles that thou doest, except God be with him.*
>
> *3. Jesus answered and said unto him, Verily, verily, I say unto thee, Except a man be born again, he cannot see the kingdom of God.*
>
> *4. Nicodemus saith unto him, How can a man be born when he is old? can he enter the second time into his mother's womb, and be born?*
>
> *5. Jesus answered, Verily, verily, I say unto thee, Except a man be born of water and of the Spirit, he cannot enter into the kingdom of God.*
>
> *6. That which is born of the flesh is flesh; and that which is born of the Spirit is spirit.*

CHAPTER 4: WHAT IS NECESSARY TO UNDERSTAND SCRIPTURE

7. Marvel not that I said unto thee, Ye must be born again.

Please notice Who it is that is doing the speaking here. It is JESUS HIMSELF! As this man named Nicodemus came to Jesus to ask Him some questions, Jesus went right to the heart of he matter and told Nicodemus what his main problem was. His main problem was that Nicodemus fit the description of 1 Corinthians 2:14 which again says, "But the natural man receiveth not the things of the Spirit of God: for they are foolishness unto him: neither can he know *them*, because they are spiritually discerned." We can see in John 3:4 and 9 that Nicodemus, a high ranking religious man, a Pharisee, was having a tough time understanding what Jesus was telling him. The things Jesus were saying were SPIRITUAL and Nicodemus, a natural man could not understand. Verse 4 states, "Nicodemus saith unto him, How can a man be born when he is old? can he enter the second time into his mother's womb, and be born?" Then in verse 9 Nicodemus asked, "Nicodemus answered and said unto him, How can these things be?" We will return to this section of verses momentarily, but let me show you another example found in the Bible that shows us another person having trouble understanding the Bible.

In Acts chapter 8 we see the account of Phillip the Evangelist and his conversation with another high ranking individual about the Scriptures. **Acts 8:26-38** says,

> *"And the angel of the Lord spake unto Philip, saying, Arise, and go toward the south unto the way that goeth down from Jerusalem unto Gaza, which is desert.*
>
> *27 And he arose and went: and, behold, a man of Ethiopia, an eunuch of great authority under Candace queen of the Ethiopians, who had the charge of all her treasure, and had come to Jerusalem for to worship,*

28 Was returning, and sitting in his chariot read Esaias the prophet.

29 Then the Spirit said unto Philip, Go near, and join thyself to this chariot.

30 And Philip ran thither to him, and heard him read the prophet Esaias, and said, Understandest thou what thou readest?

31 And he said, How can I, except some man should guide me? And he desired Philip that he would come up and sit with him.

32 The place of the scripture which he read was this, He was led as a sheep to the slaughter; and like a lamb dumb before his shearer, so opened he not his mouth:

33 In his humiliation his judgment was taken away: and who shall declare his generation? for his life is taken from the earth.

34 And the eunuch answered Philip, and said, I pray thee, of whom speaketh the prophet this? of himself, or of some other man?

35 Then Philip opened his mouth, and began at the same scripture, and preached unto him Jesus.

36 And as they went on their way, they came unto a certain water: and the eunuch said, See, here is water; what doth hinder me to be baptized?

37 And Philip said, If thou believest with all thine heart, thou mayest. And he answered and said, I believe that Jesus Christ is the Son of God.

38 And he commanded the chariot to stand still: and they went down both into the water, both Philip and the eunuch; and he baptized him.

CHAPTER 4: WHAT IS NECESSARY TO UNDERSTAND SCRIPTURE

The Ethiopian eunuch was no dummy! He had "great authority under Candace queen of the Ethiopians," he, "had charge of all her treasure," and he had gone to Jerusalem to worship. While there we suppose he had purchased a copy of Esaias (Isaiah) the prophet and was reading a certain section of it when Phillip came up to him. Phillip asked this important man, **"Understandest thou what thou readest?"** Here again is another well-educated man having a tough time understanding the things of the Spirit of God. He answered Phillip, **"How can I, except some man should guide me?"** After Phillip read the verses and explained them a little the Ethiopian eunuch asked in confusion, **"I pray thee, of whom speaketh the prophet this? of himself, or of some other man?"** Then Phillip answered him, **"and began at the same scripture, and preached unto him Jesus."** Then when the Ethiopian man asked to be baptized Phillip answered him with, "And Philip said, If thou believest with all thine heart, thou mayest." To which the eunuch said, ", I believe that Jesus Christ is the Son of God." Because a man who had the Spirit of God explained the Scripture to this man, the Ethiopian eunuch man understood and was saved and baptized right then and there. By the way, another side note, in the Alexandrian versions like the ASV, RSV and others, verse 37 IS NOT IN THERE! IT IS TOTALLY LEFT OUT! So, here is another example of a NATURAL man not receiving the things of the Spirit of God. Educated, but without understanding. Now back to John 3 and Jesus conversation with another well-educated man who was confused.

When Nicodemus asked those questions Jesus again cut to the quick with the now famous verses 3 and 5. Let's look at them here.

John 3:3,

> *"Jesus answered and said unto him, Verily, verily, I say unto thee, Except a man be born again, he cannot see the kingdom of God."*

John 3:5,

> "Jesus answered, Verily, verily, I say unto thee, Except a man be born of water and of the Spirit, he cannot enter into the kingdom of God."

Let me break THESE verses down for you…

- Jesus said this religious leader must be BORN AGAIN! Nicodemus was confused and asked, "How can a man be born when he is old? can he enter the second time into his mother's womb, and be born? Here is a natural man not understanding a Spiritual principle, Ye must be born again. How can a man be born again? Jesus answer…
- Except a man be born of water (that is the natural birth) and *of* the Spirit, (that is the Spiritual birth or being born again) he cannot enter into the kingdom of God.

Now we see why a person, even with a great education, CANNOT receive, or understand, the things of the Spirit of God. The reason is simple; **_there must be a birth of the Spirit in a man by faith in Christ to be able to understand the things of the Spirit of God. You MUST BE BORN AGAIN!_**

Before you go any further in this book answer this question in your heart…ARE YOU BORN AGAIN? If not, why not bow your head right now confessing your sinfulness and asking God to forgive you and trust Jesus Christ, and Him alone and what He did on the cross when He died to pay for all your sins to save you, and give you eternal life so you can not only go to heaven one day, but truly understand the Bible because you have not only been born of the flesh, but born of the Spirit!

Section 3

Inspiration

Theopneustos
Θεόπνευστος

"This is not what God did TO the Scriptures,

But how God GAVE the Scriptures."

Dr. Gary L. Mann

Chapter 5

𝕿𝖍𝖊 𝕮𝖆𝖘𝖊 𝖋𝖔𝖗 "𝕲𝖔𝖉-𝕭𝖗𝖊𝖆𝖙𝖍𝖊𝖉!"

Theopneustos
Θεόπνευστος

2 Timothy 3:16 & 17

> *"All scripture is given by inspiration of God, and is profitable for doctrine, for reproof, for correction, for instruction in righteousness: That the man of God may be perfect, throughly furnished unto all good works."*

The word above spelled, "theopneustos" is the English pronunciation of the Greek word "**Θεόπνευστος**." According to the Strong's Concordance it is pronounced, *theh-op'-nyoo-stos*. Second Timothy 3:16 says, *"All scripture is given by inspiration of God..."* This section of the verse tells us:

- What is inspired by God – all Scripture
- How God GAVE us all Scripture – by inspiration
- Who GAVE us all Scripture – God.

Going back to my opening statement, which will be repeated many times throughout this material, "Inspiration is not what God did to the Scriptures, but how God GAVE us the Scriptures." If it was what He did to the Scriptures, in agreement with how some teach it, it would have said, All Scripture is given TO inspiration instead of given BY inspiration!

This part of the verse uses three words in the Greek.

- πασα (pasa) meaning all
- γραφη (graf-ay) meaning Holy Writ or Scripture
- θεοπνευστος (theh-op-nyoo-stos) meaning divinely breathed or God inspired.

CHAPTER 5: THE CASE FOR "GOD-BREATHED!"

And here is where good company parts! Good company parts over the definition of inspiration. To properly understand this word that was translated inspiration I first of all want to take the Greek word apart. This must be done because to get at the correct English word the translators had to look at the Greek word first and then find its corresponding word in the English language. The Greek word theopneustos is divided into three sections.

- Theo – coming from the Greek word Theos meaning God
- Pneus – coming from the Greek word pneo meaning to breathe and,
- Tos the ending of the Greek word showing a certain type of action.

All this is vital to the conversation on the word inspiration and must be looked at carefully. But before I get to all that detail let me go back to my statement, "Inspiration is not what God did to the Scriptures, but how God GAVE us the Scriptures." The argument deals with the word inspiration and whether it tells us what God did TO the Scriptures or how God GAVE the Scriptures.

John Gill wrote about 2 Timothy 3:16,

"That is, all holy Scripture; for of that only the apostle is speaking; and he means the whole of it; not only the books of the Old Testament, but of the New, the greatest part of which was now written; for this second epistle to Timothy is by some thought to be the last of Paul's epistles; and this also will hold good of what was to be written; **for all is inspired by God, or breathed by him: the Scriptures are the breath of God, the word of God and not men;...**"

In order to understand the process God used I often say that the difference between the men God used to give the

Scriptures to and the men of Hampton Court is a blank piece of paper. Moses, David, Matthew, Paul, John and all the other men God used to write the originals did not know what God wanted them to write or say. They had the proverbial blank piece of paper in front of them...and then God spoke telling them what to write! All scripture is GIVEN by inspiration of God! Then those originals were copied and recopied through time until they were then used by the men of Hampton Court to translate the Word of God into the English language, "...with the former translations diligently compared and revised..." The men of Hampton Court (the translators of the King James Bible), had the Greek, Hebrew and Aramaic parchments to work from but it started out as a blank piece of paper with Moses and the rest of the men God used to write the Scriptures. You must remember, all Scripture is GIVEN by inspiration of God and Holy men of God spake as the Holy Spirit moved them. (2 Timothy 3:16 and 2 Peter 1:21)

The King James translators wrote in their letter to the readers in the front of many Bibles, "... (we) set before us the Hebrew and Greek to translate from the original languages." And then again, "If truth be to be tried by these things (Hebrew and Greek), then whence should a translation be made, but out of them. These tongues therefore (the Scriptures, we say, in those tongues) we set before us to translate being the tongues wherein **God was pleased to speak to His church by His prophets and Apostles."** Herein, the men of Hampton Court recognized inspiration as being how God GAVE the Scriptures...they were God-breathed! The foundational Greek word they had the responsibility to translate concerning inspiration is, as has already been mentioned, the word theopneustos. A word some are totally ignoring as you will see later.

Immediately upon looking at this word, being the Greek scholars that they were, they saw the three parts as I have laid out above and they understood what they meant and why the previous translators of the New Testament put in the word inspiration as their translation of the Greek word theopneustos.

CHAPTER 5: THE CASE FOR "GOD-BREATHED!"

They saw and understood the root words as being "theos, "pneo," and "tos." When they saw the "tos" at the end of the word and that "theo" was the beginning they understood that the "tos" was showing the action in the word as being in the **PASSIVE** tense and not in the **ACTIVE**. In his book entitled, Our God Breathed Book – The Bible, on page 50, Dr. John R. Rice quotes Ed Young concerning the ending of the word theopneustos. Mr. Young wrote,

> "The word which for our purpose is of supreme importance is the word theopneustos, translated in the English bible, "inspired of God." It is a compound, consisting of the elements theo (God) and pneustos (breathed). Now, it is well to note that the word ends in the three letters – tos. In the Greek language, words that (1) end in tos and (2) are compound with theo (God) are generally passive in meaning...(and gives the idea) that the words were "breathed by God."

He goes on to say,

> "...there have been those who have somewhat vigorously insisted that the meaning is ACTIVE. They would therefore translate by the phrase "breathing out God" in the sense that the Scriptures breathed forth or were imbued with the Spirit of God. Such, however, as has been noted above, is not the true meaning. The true meaning is passive, "that which is breathed out by God." Another way to understand this is that the Active tense would mean it is continuously being breathed while the passive tense means it has already been breathed, or spoken, by God. In other words, when God spoke the words of the Word of God, it was done! This all has to do with some who believe in dual and even triple inspiration which is not accurate. When God spoke the words

of the Word of God to Moses and all the other writers of the Scriptures all the way through John, there was no more to add to it. It was passive and not active. More will be said about this in later chapters and will be made abundantly clear.

In the same book on page 51 it continues with,

> "The Scriptures therefore are the writing which found their origin with God: **they are the very product of His creative breath….**According to Paul, the Scriptures are not writings into which something Divine has been breathed (it is not what God did to the Scriptures, but how God gave the Scriptures); they are not writings which are imbued with the Divine Spirit. The Scriptures, Paul vigorously asserts, are writing which **came into being because they were breathed out by God Himself.**"

A.T. Fausset wrote,

> "What it says of Scripture is, not that it was breathed into by God, or is the product of the inbreathing of God into the human writers, but that it is breathed out by God. God breathed, the product of the creative breath of God."

There are a few today who say that what God did was to breath into the Scriptures, but this is not so! There are also those who deny the definition of inspiration as meaning "God breathed." But they are wrong! God breathed, or spoke the words of the Word of God. Remember, this is why the Scriptures are called the Word of God!

The following are taken from different Bibles that the translators could have looked at in their work of translation which shows that 2 Timothy 3:16 all have the word theopneustos to be translated inspiration.

CHAPTER 5: THE CASE FOR "GOD-BREATHED!"

Geneva Bible – "For the whole Scripture is geuen by inspiration of God…"

Bishops Bible – "All scripture is geuen by inspiration of God…"

Not only did the translators know Greek and Hebrew, but they also knew Latin which is the basis for most of the English language. Some today are critical of the definition "God breathed" because they have their own definition which totally ignores the etymology of the word inspiration and the Latin. From the etymology of the word inspiration from the 1300's is this definition, "the immediate influence of God, especially that under which the holy books were written." The Old French gives the meaning for inspiration as, "inhaling, breathing." From the Latin "inspirare," meaning to inspire, influence, to blow or breathe from the different parts of the word,

- In - meaning in, and
- Spirar – meaning to breathe
- Tion – this indicates an active process, state or result.

The literal sense of the word then is the "act of inhaling" attested from the 1560's. Remembering that inspiration is not what God did TO the Scriptures but how God GAVE the Scriptures, you can then understand that the act of inhaling had to do with God speaking because you must inhale to speak. Besides the fact of what the Bible says over, and over, and over when it says things like, "Thus saith the Lord!"

In the criticism of the definition "God breathed," some will say that the English corrects the Greek. (More will be said about that later also.) But they totally ignore the Latin and the definition which the word inspiration comes from. But, an honest rendering of the word theopneustos, which is what the translators, the men of Hampton Court, were assigned with, and all the previous translators before them, who, unlike the critics of today, knew Greek, Hebrew and Latin, shows us that they translated it to the word inspiration and is totally in agreement with the definition of "God breathed." The critics say the "spir" in inspiration means Spirit and their definition is the action of the Spirit in the words. But, I am getting a little ahead of myself again.

Another part of their criticism comes from their objection of the Strong's Concordance with the Greek "pneo" which the Strong's Concordance points to as the "presumed derivative" making it the Greek word that the other forms come from. They try to teach that the Greek word "pneo" is not what the "pneus" in theopneustos comes from. Rather, they teach that instead of "pneus" coming from "pneo" it really comes from "pneuma" making it the presumed derivitave. Again disagreeing with those in history who KNEW the Greek as opposed to those today who do not! They do not agree with the definition "God breathed." But then they have to strain and totally ignore both the Greek and the Latin and the scholarship of all the past translators. These critics do not like the definition "God breathed," and they base this on the "presumed derivative" statement of the Strong's Concordance. Well, if the man who wrote the book and who also knew the Greek better than the critics who do not know the Greek says that "pneo" is the word the others come from, then I reckon that "pneuma" is NOT! I can play chess and I know the man who wrote the book on chess. What the critics of the men of Hampton Court and Strong's Concordance are trying to do is say those men are wrong and they are right. It would be like me telling the man who wrote a book on chess that he is wrong. I guarantee he could run circles around me if I were to play him a game of chess and the men who knew the Greek, Hebrew and Latin languages fluently can make us look mighty ignorant! Plus, I looked it up in another lexicon and "pneuma" is the derivative of ……… wait for it………drum roll please…….what's behind that door……. "PNEO." In other words the Greek word "pneuma" **comes from** the Greek word "pneo" making it the word the others are derived from. Would you like to guess what "pneo" means? (I hear another drum roll), it means, "TO BREATHE!" Theopneustos

CHAPTER 5: THE CASE FOR "GOD-BREATHED!"

and inspiration are both talking about God breathing as He gave us the words to the Word of God! The Bible is **God breathed!** All Scripture is given (passive not active) by God's breath! God breathed all Scripture! This is the process of how God GAVE the Scripture!

In one man's writings is the following,

> "The word inspiration in 2 Timothy 3:16 is literally defined in the other verses that we just read above (referring to Acts 7:38 an; John 6:63). The word inspiration DOES NOT MEAN GOD BREATHED, BUT IT MEANS GOD'S WORDS ARE SPIRIT."

But this totally ignores the Greek and the Latin! This "definition" is not based on looking up the word but is based on, "… (using) the Bible to TRY AND FIGURE OUT what God is trying to tell us when it comes to His Word…" What is so wrong with looking up words in a dictionary or lexicon? What is wrong with using the SAME definitions of those before us who knew Greek?

In an online Bible college lesson on the inspiration of the Bible, the teacher made this comment,

> "Years ago, the word (inspiration) was INCORRECTLY DEFINED, GOD-BREATHED! It seemed like a good definition that we got from our Greek lexicon, and THAT DEFINITION WON THE ARGUMENT OF THE DAY! The old battle the fundamentalists fought was, is the Bible written by thought inspiration or verbal inspiration? The modernist believes that God gave the thoughts and then they wrote it down in their own words. John R. Rice and others believed that God gave man the words and that the Bible was God-breathed. THAT WAS GOOD FOR THAT DAY, BUT TODAY AFTER LOOKING AT IT

MORE DEEPLY (with no study in the Greek or Latin or using dictionaries or lexicons – my statement), AND SEEING MAN TAKE THAT DEFINITION TO ITS LOGICAL CONCLUSION, THE DEFINITION IS FOUND FALTERING."

Well, no it isn't found faltering; their process to come up with the NEW definition is what is found faltering! God DID give us His Word VERBALLY! That means He gave us the Word by speaking it which is what verbal inspiration is! From Webster's 1828 Dictionary is the definition for "VERBAL"

VERB'AL, a. [L. verbalis.]

1**. Spoken; expressed to the ear in words;** not written; as a verbal message; a verbal contract; verbal testimony.

2. Oral; uttered by the mouth.

We still believe in **VERBAL INSPIRATION!** GOD-BREATHED!

Above he said,

> "...that definition (God-breathed) won the argument of the day..."

Meaning that the CORRECT definition of "God-breathed," backed VERBAL INSPIRATION! Just because the "argument" has changed does not mean the definition has changed! He also stated, "That (definition) good for that day..." again meaning it was CORRECT then. Well, what was correct then, what was good for that day that won the argument IS STILL GOOD TODAY!

No! Our understanding of the Greek or English words have not advanced as the critics teach, especially when the same teacher said that the Hebrew and Greek languages are, "...old, dead languages!" He also advocates the teaching that we are not to study these "old and dead" languages at all and doing so will

CHAPTER 5: THE CASE FOR "GOD-BREATHED!"

somehow corrupt you. He then made mention of John R. Rice inferring that "those older men" fell for the incorrect definitions found in their lexicons. Yet this teacher said that it was the correct definition for that day! What confusion! I prefer to quote my Greek teacher in class who said, "Never say it is Greek to me mocking the language God chose to give us the Word of God through." I prefer to teach the SAME things from the "older men."

The argument mentioned above about not using lexicons etc. is a weak argument. They say we are not to use them because they were written by sinful men! The same person who said that is a sinful man too, should we listen to him? The man writing this sentence is a sinful man and the preacher who expounds the Word of God to his people is a sinful man. Are we not to read ANY books or listen to ANY preaching done by sinful men? That is ridiculous!

Their argument continues that men like John R. Rice and others have been influenced in a wrong way by the Strong's concordance and others. The Strong's Concordance was first published in 1890. I wonder what those BEFORE the lexicons said about inspiration? Let's go back into the middle 1700's to a Baptist named John Gill and see what he said.

In referring to 2 Timothy 3:16 he wrote,

"That is, all holy Scripture; for of that only the apostle is speaking; and he means the whole of it; not only the books of the Old Testament, but of the New, the greatest part of which was now written; for this second epistle to Timothy is by some thought to be the last of Paul's epistles; and this also will hold good of what was to be written; **for all is inspired by God, or breathed by him: the Scriptures are the breath of God, the word of God and not men;**..."

AND WHAT MARVEL!

Sounds to me like he meant the Scriptures were God-breathed!

Spurgeon in his message on Isaiah 1:20 entitled,

> "The Infallibility of the Scriptures" which was preached in 1888, BEFORE he could be ruined by the Strong's Concordance said, "What Isaiah said was, therefore spoken by Jehovah. It was audibly the utterance of a man, but, really, it was the utterance of the Lord Himself. The lips which delivered the words were those of Isaiah, but yet it was the very truth that, The mouth of the Lord has spoken it. ALL SCRIPTURE, BEING INSPIRED OF THE SPIRIT **IS <u>SPOKEN BY THE MOUTH OF GOD!</u>**"

Sounds to me like he meant the Scriptures were God-breathed!

They were not influenced by liberals or modernists! They had not fallen for the "wrong definitions" found in lexicons. Those men knew their Greek, they understood the English and Latin and they believed that inspiration was speaking about all Scripture being "God-breathed!" God SPOKE the words of the Word of God! Inspiration is not what God did to the Scriptures it is how God GAVE the Scriptures.

Herbert Lockyer in his work "<u>All the Doctrines of the Bible</u>" published by Zondervan Publishers said,

> "The particular word used by Paul means God-Breathed!" That is God Himself or through the Holy Spirit TOLD THE WRITERS OF THE BIBLE THE VERY THINGS TO RECORD." (Page 7, 8)

J. Vernon McGee in his work "<u>Through the Bible</u>" wrote,

> The word inspiration means, God-breathed." (Volume 5, page 473)

CHAPTER 5: THE CASE FOR "GOD-BREATHED!"

W.E. Vines "<u>Expository Dictionary of New Testament Words</u>" wrote,

> "Theopneustos inspired of God (theos – God; pneo – to breathe). Wycliff, Tyndale, Coverdale and the Great Bible have the rendering, "inspired of God." (Page 263)

John R. Rice in his book, "<u>Our God Breathed Book – The Bible</u>" wrote on page 48,

> "a fundamental statement of Scripture about inspiration is in 2 Timothy 3:16. The Scriptures are breathed out by God!"

He also wrote on page 49,

> "…the meaning in the original Greek, theopneustos, is much more definite. It is literally God-breathed. All Scripture is "God-breathed,"

that is, the Scripture itself is breathed out from God. God is its origin. The miracle of the Scriptures came directly from God."

Shelton Smith in his book entitled, "<u>The Book We Call the Bible</u>" wrote,

> "The word for inspiration in the Greek text is theopneustos. It means "God-breathed." Now that simply means the actual words of Scripture are the fruit of His very own breath…in this context of creating Scripture, it doesn't just mean that God exuded His influence on it, but it means that He breathed out words…He gave each of the writers His very own words!"

Mickey Carter in his book, "<u>Things That Are Different Are Not the Same</u>," on page 17 wrote, "…inspired – God-breathed." Then on page 74 he wrote the following, "Word for word, the very minute details (jots and tittles), were God-breathed."

Roy Branson in his work entitled, "Most Christians Don't Know What Every Christian Should Know" wrote on page 21,

"God was the mind, the writers were the mouth."

David Sorenson in "God's Perfect Book" published in 2009 wrote,

"It is significant to note, that it is the Scriptures which were inspired…What they wrote were words – the very basic vehicle of thought created by God Himself. As any serious student of the Bible knows, the term theopneustos is comprised of 2 smaller words, theos and pneustos which literally means, "God- breathed." Then the Bible is a God spoken book." (Pages 28 and 29)

Bill Grady in his work "Final Authority" wrote on page 16,

"…inspiration describes the singular act when God mysteriously breathed out the very words…"

R. B. Ouellette wrote in "A More Sure Word" on page 30,

"Inspiration means God-breathed." Also on that page he quotes Charles Ryrie who said, "The Bible originates as an action of God who breathed it out."

Again, Shelton Smith, the Editor of the Sword of the Lord was quoted in the July/August 2008 edition of the "Baptist Magazine,"

"When we say it (the Bible) was given by inspiration of God, we mean that God Himself gave us His own words. (Page 23)

Dr. Jack Hyles in his book, Meet the Holy Spirit wrote on page 13,

CHAPTER 5: THE CASE FOR "GOD-BREATHED!"

"God breathed His Word TO man. (Notice he did not say God breathed into the Word!) The term Holy Spirit could easily be stated Holy breath. Thus, the Holy Spirit, a Holy breath, moved upon man and GOD BREATHED HIS BOOK TO MAN. GOD SPOKE TO MOSES AND TOLD HIM WHAT TO WRITE. He spoke, In the beginning and Moses wrote, In the beginning….Some man made scholars shout, "But that is mechanical dictation." No, that's verbal inspiration. The eternal Word of God was given word by word to holy men of old as the Holy Spirit breathed the Word of God TO them and upon them." Sounds to me he believed in God-breathed and in verbal inspiration, as do I!

Inspiration is not what God did to the Scriptures; inspiration is how God Gave the Scriptures. **The Scriptures are the words of God, they are God-breathed!** I will teach the same things thank you very much!

Verses to Consider

2 Samuel 23:2

The Spirit of the LORD spake by me, and his word was in my tongue.

1 Kings 12:22

But the word of God came unto Shemaiah the man of God, saying,

1 Kings 12:23

Speak unto Rehoboam, the son of Solomon, king of Judah, and unto all the house of Judah and Benjamin, and to the remnant of the people, saying,

1 Kings 21:17

> *And the word of the LORD came to Elijah the Tishbite, saying,*

Psalm 33:6

> *By the word of the LORD were the heavens made; and all the host of them by the breath of his mouth.*

Psalm 68:11

> *The Lord gave the word: great was the company of those that published it.*

Psalm 119:88

> *Quicken me after thy lovingkindness; so shall I keep the testimony of thy mouth.*

Psalm 138:4

> *All the kings of the earth shall praise thee, O LORD, when they hear the words of thy mouth.*

Isaiah 55:11

> *So shall my word be that goeth forth out of my mouth: it shall not return unto me void, but it shall accomplish that which I please, and it shall prosper in the thing whereto I sent it.*

Jeremiah 1:4

> *Then the word of the LORD came unto me, saying,*

Ezekiel 11:5

> *And the Spirit of the LORD fell upon me, and said unto me, Speak; Thus saith the LORD; Thus have ye said, O house of Israel: for I know the things that come into your mind, every one of them.*

CHAPTER 5: THE CASE FOR "GOD-BREATHED!"

1 Thessalonians 2:13

> *For this cause also thank we God without ceasing, because, when ye received the word of God which ye heard of us, ye received it not as the word of men, but as it is in truth, the word of God, which effectually worketh also in you that believe.*

The critics of "God breathed," have said,

"This is their premise (those of us who still believe that inspiration means "God breathed") and if their premise is true that God did not speak in English, then technically they are right...God did not breathe out in English, therefore if inspiration means God breathed then we don't have an inspired Bible."

What rubbish, this totally ignores the Greek, Latin and the process of preservation in translation.

I even went back into the Latin and French and studied the etymology of the word inspiration and found that the "spir" in the word inspiration comes from the Latin "spirare" which is not talking about the spirit but which again means to breathe; to inhale and then exhale as in speaking.

Inspiration is the original act of God speaking His Word to the writers of the books of the Bible, who then spoke what God said and wrote what He said. Inspiration is how God gave us all Scripture, not what He did to all Scripture! All Scripture is GIVEN (how?) by inspiration of God.

Chapter 6

The Holy Spirit and God's Word

2 Peter 1:12 - 21

Wherefore I will not be negligent to put you always in remembrance of these things, though ye know them, and be established in the present truth.

Yea, I think it meet, as long as I am in this tabernacle, to stir you up by putting you in remembrance;

Knowing that shortly I must put off this my tabernacle, even as our Lord Jesus Christ hath shewed me.

Moreover I will endeavour that ye may be able after my decease to have these things always in remembrance.

For we have not followed cunningly devised fables, when we made known unto you the power and coming of our Lord Jesus Christ, but were eyewitnesses of his majesty.

For he received from God the Father honour and glory, when there came such a voice to him from the excellent glory, This is my beloved Son, in whom I am well pleased.

And this voice which came from heaven we heard, when we were with him in the holy mount.

We have also a more sure word of prophecy; whereunto ye do well that ye take heed, as unto a light that shineth in a dark place, until the day dawn, and the day star arise in your hearts:

CHAPTER 6: THE HOLY SPIRIT AND GOD'S WORD

Knowing this first, that no prophecy of the scripture is of any private interpretation.

For the prophecy came not in old time by the will of man: but holy men of God spake as they were moved by the Holy Ghost.

In any conversation about the inspiration of the Scriptures, the Holy Spirit must have a large part of it. But, in must all be Bible centered just like any other topic having to do with the Word of God.

In 2 Peter, the realization of the Apostle Peter was, "Knowing that shortly I must put off *this* my tabernacle, even as our Lord Jesus Christ hath shewed me." He was told this in John 21:18 and 19 when Jesus told Peter, "Verily, verily, I say unto thee, When thou wast young, thou girdedst thyself, and walkedst whither thou wouldest: but when thou shalt be old, thou shalt stretch forth thy hands, and another shall gird thee, and carry *thee* whither thou wouldest not. This spake he, signifying by what death he should glorify God. And when he had spoken this, he saith unto him, Follow me." Peter at this time was sure that his death was not too far away and, as is always the case, he wanted the Christians to remember some very important things. This was stated in verses 12, 13 and 14 which say, "Wherefore I will not be negligent to put you always in remembrance of these things, though ye know *them,* and be established in the present truth. Yea, I think it meet, as long as I am in this tabernacle, to stir you up by putting *you* in remembrance; Knowing that shortly I must put off *this* my tabernacle, even as our Lord Jesus Christ hath shewed me."

What was it that Peter wanted them to, "have…always in remembrance?" He answers that in verses 16 through 21. Within those verses are some important parts of the continued teaching. First, Peter tells them what he had actually seen and heard. He wrote in verses 16 through 18,

> *"For we have not followed cunningly devised fables, when we made known unto you the power and coming of our Lord Jesus Christ, but were eyewitnesses of his majesty. For he received from God the Father honour and glory, when there came such a voice to him from the excellent glory, This is my beloved Son, in whom I am well pleased. And this voice which came from heaven we heard, when we were with him in the holy mount."*

He was on the Mount of Transfiguration when he saw Jesus glorified and heard the voice of God; he was an eyewitness of all that happened that day! Can you imagine having been there and then trying to tell others about it!

What he wrote next is very important and speaks for itself.

> *"We have also a more sure word of prophecy; whereunto ye do well that ye take heed, as unto a light that shineth in a dark place, until the day dawn, and the day star arise in your hearts:"*

He was saying that what is written in Scripture is more sure than what I can tell you I saw! Remember, he wanted them to remember these things! So, he then begins to tell all Christians about this "more sure word of prophecy!"

Then in verses 20 and 21 he was inspired to write,

> *"Knowing this first, that no prophecy of the scripture is of any private interpretation. For the prophecy came not in old time by the will of man: but holy men of God spake **as they were moved by the Holy Ghost.**"*

Here are some other verses dealing with this...

CHAPTER 6: THE HOLY SPIRIT AND GOD'S WORD

1 Samuel 10:10 *And when they came thither to the hill, behold, a company of prophets met him; and the Spirit of God came upon him, and he prophesied among them.*

Ezekiel 2:2 *And the spirit entered into me when he spake unto me, and set me upon my feet, that I heard him that spake unto me.*

Ezekiel 11:5 *And the Spirit of the LORD fell upon me, and said unto me, Speak; Thus saith the LORD; Thus have ye said, O house of Israel: for I know the things that come into your mind, every one of them.*

God has always communicated with men. Back in the Garden of Eden God communicated personally with Adam and Eve as found in Genesis 1:28-30; 2:16 & 17 and 3:8 through 19. Then of course, there are hundreds of places (413 to be exact) in the Bible that uses the phrase, "Thus saith the Lord!" The phrase, "The Word of the Lord" is used in 255 verses where God communicates with mankind. The vehicle He always used was words! We see His method of communication in Hebrews 1:1 and 2 which states,

> *"God, who at sundry times and in divers manners **spake** in time past unto the fathers by the prophets, Hath in these last days **spoken** unto us by his Son, whom he hath appointed heir of all things, by whom also he made the worlds;"*

An interesting thing to point out here is, as was mentioned above, His method of communicating with man has almost always been through SPEAKING! This agrees with the correct definition of theopneustos which is "God-breathed!" The inspiration of Scripture is NOT that God breathed INTO the Scripture, but that He BREATHED SCRIPTURE as He spoke them to the writers. The King James translators and previous translations were correct in their translation of theopneustos when they wrote, "all Scripture is GIVEN by inspiration of God!" The inspiration of Scriptures is not the Holy Spirit living in the Scriptures as some teach, and inspiration is not to be defined as "the acts of the Holy Spirit IN the Scripture." The definition of inspiration is God-breathed or God spoke THROUGH the Holy Spirit. It is also interesting to note that the Trinity has all been active in the communication with mankind.

The Holy Spirit and the Word of God are inseparable. The life or power of the Scriptures is the power of the Holy Spirit as He backs the Scriptures. It is not that He indwells the Scriptures as the breath of God. Dr. Jack Hyles in his book <u>Meet the Holy Spirit</u> wrote on pages 13,

> "The Holy Spirit **speaks from the outside through His Word and then He speaks from the inside (of us) as He confirms His preached Word to the hearer.**"

On pages 14 and 15 he wrote,

> "...He who breathed the Book to us through holy men of old can sit beside us as we study it, and He will teach things not on the surface."

Again, inspiration is not what God did to the Scriptures; it is how He gave the Scriptures and the Holy Spirit Who indwells us teaches us what the Scriptures say, not because He is IN them, but because He is in us. This is why the Bible is called the Sword of the Spirit in Ephesians 6:17.

> *"And take the helmet of salvation, and the sword of the Spirit, which is the word of God:"*

A very good example of this is found in Luke 24:32 which states,

> *"And they said one to another, Did not our heart burn within us, while he talked with us by the way, and while he opened to us the scriptures?"*

Gill wrote about this verse,

> "The Scriptures are as a sealed book to men, learned and unlearned; and none so fit to open

CHAPTER 6: THE HOLY SPIRIT AND GOD'S WORD

them as the lion of the tribe of Judah: he did open and explain them to these his disciples, as well as conversed with them about other things, as they travelled together; and his words came with such evidence, power, and sweetness, that they were ravished with them; their minds were irradiated with beams and rays of divine light; their hearts were warmed and glowed within them; they became fervent in spirit, and their affections were raised and fired; they found the word to be as burning fire within them; and they now knew somewhat what it was to be baptized with fire, which is Christ's peculiar office to administer; see Psa 39:3 they seem as it were not only to reflect on these things with wonder and pleasure, but also to charge themselves with want of thought, with inattention and stupidity; since they might have concluded from the uncommon evidence, force, and energy with which his words came to them, who he was, seeing no man could speak as he did, and with such effect as his words had."

As the Lord spoke to the men on the road to Emmaus, He taught them about the things that had happened in Jerusalem and there was power behind what He taught them from the Scriptures. That power is the Holy Spirit! This is why an unsaved man cannot understand the things of God because the things of God are SPIRTUALLY DISCERNED! (See the chapter on why a person needs to be saved to understand the Word of God!)

Albert Barnes wrote about verse 32,

"It is proper there should be those whose office it is to explain the Scriptures. Jesus did it while on earth; **he does it now by his Spirit**; and he has appointed his ministers, whose business it is to explain them."

Again, this agrees with why a person must be born again (of the water and of the SPIRIT), In 1 Corinthians 2:10-16 it tells us the Word of God is SPIRITUALLY DISCERNED and that an unsaved person who does not have the Spirit of God CANNOT receive or know them because he is not indwelt by the Spirit of God which comes at salvation! While there are clear verses which tell us that at salvation we receive and are sealed by the Holy Spirit, there are no clear verses saying the Holy Spirit indwells the Word of God! It is only assumed!

In 1 Peter 1:23 when it says,

"Being born again, not of corruptible seed, but of incorruptible, by the word of God, which liveth and abideth for ever,"

It has been assumed that the Word of God is alive because of the Holy Spirits indwelling of the Word of God. Nowhere in this verse does it say that. But, this verse clearly teaches that the Word of God liveth and abideth forever because GOD lives and abides forever! In his commentary on this verse John Gill wrote, "...he phrases, "which liveth and abideth forever", may be either read in connection only with "God", and as descriptive of him, who is the living God, is from everlasting to everlasting, in distinction from idols; and here added, to show that he can give power and efficacy to his word, to regenerate and quicken, and will continue to preserve and make it useful to all his saving purposes;" As I have said in another work of mine, the life of the Word of God depends on the life of the God of the Word of God! Since God is forever, then His Word is forever!

We are regenerated, or, born again, when we place our total faith in Christ. The Holy Spirit uses the Word of God to convict or convince us of sin and our need of salvation using the Word of God. Then the Holy Spirit indwells us making it possible for us then to receive the things of the Spirit of God, the Word of God. Since we now have the Spirit of God dwelling in us, then He uses the Word of God in our lives, not because the

CHAPTER 6: THE HOLY SPIRIT AND GOD'S WORD

Holy Spirit dwells in the Bible, but because He dwells in us! Let me put it this way, Now that I know the author who lives with me, I can understand His writings! Without the indwelling of the Spirit of God in my life, I cannot understand His Writings!

In Isaiah 59:21 we see the connection between the Spirit and the Word of God. It says,

> *"As for me, this is my covenant with them, saith the LORD;* **My spirit that is upon thee, and my words which I have put in thy mouth,** *shall not depart out of thy mouth, nor out of the mouth of thy seed, nor out of the mouth of thy seed's seed, saith the LORD, from henceforth and for ever."*

The Holy Spirit is here connected to the Word of God and He uses the Word of God in our lives. He will always totally agree with the words of the Word of God because they are spiritually discerned! He gave them, He uses them.

The verse in John 6:63 which says,

> *"It is the spirit that quickeneth; the flesh profiteth nothing: the words that I speak unto you, they are spirit, and they are life,"*

is also used by some assuming, based on their wrong definition of inspiration, that the Holy Spirit lives in the Word of God because it says that, "they (the Words) are spirit and they are life." This is not the correct interpretation for this verse. Jesus was teaching some very important and difficult things in John 6:22-68. First, He begins to teach about His being the bread of life! They asked the question in verse 28, "What shall we do, that we might work the works of God?" They were not sure who He was speaking of so He took it a step further with verse 35 where He stated that HE WAS THE BREAD OF LIFE! His teaching was that they were to believe in Him and that He was the Bread of life!

Then, of course comes verses 41 and 42 which states, "The Jews then murmured at him, because he said, I am the bread which came down from heaven. And they said, Is not this Jesus, the son of Joseph, whose father and mother we know? how is it then that he saith, I came down from heaven?" Always remember that the preaching of the cross is to them that perish foolishness. These people were greatly offended that He said He was that bread. Remember, He is speaking, or, communicating with people. To their doubts He responded, "Jesus therefore answered and said unto them, Murmur not among yourselves. No man can come to me, except the Father which hath sent me draw him: and I will raise him up at the last day. It is written in the prophets, And they shall be all taught of God. Every man therefore that hath heard, and hath learned of the Father, cometh unto me. Not that any man hath seen the Father, save he which is of God, he hath seen the Father. Verily, verily, I say unto you, He that believeth on me hath everlasting life. I am that bread of life. Your fathers did eat manna in the wilderness, and are dead. This is the bread which cometh down from heaven, that a man may eat thereof, and not die. I am the living bread which came down from heaven: if any man eat of this bread, he shall live for ever: and the bread that I will give is my flesh, which I will give for the life of the world." He was teaching them a SPIRITUAL lesson on Who He was and how they could be saved. His words were LIFE GIVING!

Then the really hard part for them came when in verse 51 He said,

> *"I am the living bread which came down from heaven: if any man eat of this bread, he shall live for ever: and the bread that I will give is my flesh, which I will give for the life of the world."*

They did not understand that He was talking about His death where He would give His body and blood. They thought, "...How can this man give us *his* flesh to eat?" They thought He was speaking about cannibalism! They totally did not understand His words, what He was saying, were about His crucifixion and that whoever would trusts totally in His sacrifice could be saved!

CHAPTER 6: THE HOLY SPIRIT AND GOD'S WORD

Then in verses 60 through 62 we see,

> *"Many therefore of his disciples, when they had heard this, said, This is an hard saying; who can hear it? When Jesus knew in himself that his disciples murmured at it, he said unto them, Doth this offend you? What and if ye shall see the Son of man ascend up where he was before?"*

He then explains to them He was saying in verse 63 which says,

> *"It is the spirit that quickeneth; the flesh profiteth nothing: the words that I speak unto you, they are spirit, and they are life."*

Now, if you leave out all the above you could come to an incorrect understanding of this verse. You must always look at the verses before and after a verse to totally understand a teaching. But, if you ignore those verses and ignore what others in history have taught about this verse, you might agree with the teaching that uses verse 63 to teach the Spirit indwells the Scriptures and that the breath of God in the Scriptures is what makes them alive. In their teaching about this I have witnessed a preacher say that the Word of God actually breathes! Now the living Word Jesus does, but the Book we call the Bible does not!

What do some from history teach about this verse?

John Gill –

> "...it is the Spirit of God that quickens dead sinners, by entering into them as the spirit of life, and causing them to live: and it is spiritual eating, or eating the flesh, and drinking the blood of Christ in a spiritual sense, which quickens, refreshes, and comforts the minds of believers; it is that by, and on which they live,... **the words that I speak unto you,** *they* **are spirit, and** *they* **are life**; the doctrines which Christ had then been

delivering concerning himself, his flesh and blood, being spiritually understood, are the means of quickening souls. The Gospel, and the truths of it, which are the wholesome words of our Lord Jesus Christ, are the means of conveying the Spirit of God, as a spirit of illumination and sanctification, into the hearts of men, and of quickening sinners dead in trespasses and sins: the Gospel is the Spirit that giveth life, and is the savour of life unto life, when it comes not in word only, or in the bare ministry of it, but with the energy of the Holy Ghost, and the power of divine grace."

The others I have read all pretty much agree with John Gill, and so do I! The literal eating of His flesh and drinking of His blood would do nothing and Jesus was not telling them it would. They would be just as lost as before. But, a SPIRITUAL application of this teaching would bring life, everlasting life! THAT is what is being taught here. His words are spirit and life. Notice, it does not say that they are spirit and they are **LIVING**! It says they are spirit and they are **LIFE**!

The Holy Spirit is a vital part of the GIVING of the Word of God and is a vital part in the UNDERTANDING of the Word of God. He always uses the Scriptures to convict and teach and remind us as we use the Word of God! Remember what it is profitable for. It is profitable for doctrine, for reproof, correction and instruction that we may be perfect and thoroughly furnished unto all good works. He uses the Scriptures which are spiritually discerned, to help us see our need of salvation, that Christ is the only way of salvation and then He gently enters our lives to teach us Scripture and empower us.

NO! This verse is not teaching that the Word of God has the Spirit in it and, no, it is not teaching that it is actually breathing and alive! Its' words are Spiritual words which brings life! The Spirit of God indwells the believer, not the Scriptures. He was a part of the GIVING of them and empowers it in our

CHAPTER 6: THE HOLY SPIRIT AND GOD'S WORD

lives while we read it and listen to it preached! God give us some Spirit filled preaching and Spirit filled listening!

Chapter 7
The Efficacy of the Scriptures

(I wrote this chapter and published it in a small pamphlet back in 2012 and recently decided to copy and paste it here for this part of this book. Some of it will be repetitious but I decided to leave it exactly as I wrote it then.)

According to the Webster's 1828 dictionary, efficacy means,

> "Power to produce effects; production to the effect intended; as the efficacy of the gospel in converting men from sin; the efficacy of prayer;"

The question is, what makes the Scriptures efficacious? The word "efficacious" means,

"Effectual; productive of effects; producing the effect intended; having power adequate to the purpose intended; powerful;"

So what is it about the Bible that makes it produce the purpose intended; what helps the Scriptures to be effective in people's lives? This is the primary question I am asking in this material.

I was told in college that what we do with the Bible determines what God does with us. I have been saying for some time that if study causes us to rightly divide the word of truth, then a lack of study causes us to wrongly divide it. While all of this is true I still must ask the question, what makes the Bible effective in our lives? What causes its effectiveness?

God makes the Bible effective in our lives! In 2 Timothy 3:16 we see,

> "*All scripture is given by inspiration of* **God**, *and is profitable for doctrine, for reproof, for correction, for instruction in righteousness:*"

CHAPTER 7: THE EFFICACY OF GOD'S WORD

While much of the conversation on this verse has to do with the Holy Spirit's part in the inspiration of the Scriptures, which I will get back to later, the part of the verse that I want to emphasize is where it says, "All scripture *is* given by inspiration of **GOD**..." While the debate has been in the method of inspiration, and what is inspired, the part that has been ignored is in the original language which uses the Greek word, "theopneustos, "which means "God breathed." The argument has been against that definition but if you look at and study the etymology of the word, you will see that the word is divided into two basic words. The first is the word "THEO" which comes from the word "THEOS" which means God! The second part being "PNEO" which means, "to breathe hard." While we believe that inspiration is the influence and direction of the Holy Spirit in the giving of the words of Scripture to mankind, the history of the word I found says,

"The etymology of the word inspiration comes from the Latin "in," which means into, and "spirare," which means to breathe."

From another source, none of which have been from the recent controversial sources, the very first definition says,

<u>"The act of inspiring, of breathing into."</u> (From <u>Wiktionary</u>)

While I am on this point, let me tell you that of the 22 sources I looked into that I have in my office, 21 of them all agree that the Greek word "theopneustos" means God breathed. The point I want to make above the present controversy, is that it is **God** Who is behind the inspiration of the Scriptures. We must not ignore the word "Theos" in the Greek and it was correctly translated in the King James Bible when it says, "All scripture is given by inspiration of ***God***..." Since the history of the word inspiration means God breathed, and there is absolutely nothing wrong doctrinally with using that definition, we must center our attention not on the word breathed, but on God! He is the One

Who is instrumental in the giving of the Word of God to us. Now do not jump to conclusions, the Holy Spirit and Jesus Christ are also instrumental in the giving of the Scriptures which we will see later, but the question I am asking is not **how** did we get the Scriptures, the question is how it is effective? But, in order to understand how the Scriptures are effective, we must understand Who is behind it. A contract is only as good as the people who sign on the line so we must see who it is that is behind the Scriptures. Once we see who is behind the Scriptures, we will see how they are effective.

In today's discussion of the inspiration of the Bible, there are those who try to get their definition from the breaking down of the English word inspiration. They try to point out the "spir," in the word inspiration and say that it is referring to the Holy Spirit. Again, as we will see later, the Holy Spirit had a very important part in the inspiration of the Bible, but the translators not only knew Greek and Hebrew, but they also knew Latin! The "spir" in the English word inspiration is not from the Greek but from the Latin, which most English words are based on, and it means breathe! But let me stay with the Greek on this for a moment. Again, the word inspiration comes from the Greek word, "theopneustos." The two important parts of this word again are, "theo" and "pneustas." The latter part comes from the root word "pneo." How is "pneo" used in the Bible? There are 7 instances in Scripture on how this word is used. They are found in the following verses.

Matthew 7:25

> *"And the rain descended, and the floods came, and the winds blew (pneo), and beat upon that house; and it fell not: for it was founded upon a rock."*

CHAPTER 7: THE EFFICACY OF GOD'S WORD

Matthew 7:27

> "And the rain descended, and the floods came, and the winds blew (pneo), and beat upon that house; and it fell: and great was the fall of it."

Luke 12:55

> "And when ye see the south wind blow (pneo), ye say, There will be heat; and it cometh to pass."

John 3:8

> "The wind bloweth (pneo) where it listeth, and thou hearest the sound thereof, but canst not tell whence it cometh, and whither it goeth: so is every one that is born of the Spirit."

John 6:18

> "And the sea arose by reason of a great wind that blew (pneo)."

Acts 27:40

> "And when they had taken up the anchors, they committed themselves unto the sea, and loosed the rudder bands, and hoised up the mainsail to the wind (pneo), and made toward shore."

Revelation 7:1

> "And after these things I saw four angels standing on the four corners of the earth, holding the four winds of the earth, that the wind should not blow (pneo) on the earth, nor on the sea, nor on any tree."

We see then in every case that pneo has to do with a wind or a wind blowing. Who does that? It is the process that God started at creation. God is behind the wind and so God is behind the giving of the Word of God by His breath. So, the Greek word, "theopneustos" means GOD breathed! As God, through the Holy

Spirit, breathed the words to the Holy men of old, the men wrote them.

An interesting note here then I will move on, one person has written,

> "The Greek word there is never translated in the Bible with the word breathe – never! Never in the King James Bible – it is in the NIV." (GM, An obvious attempt to say that if you disagree with him then you agree with the NIV which we certainly do not.) Then he went on to say, "It is almost always translated as "spirit" (322 times), "Ghost" or "ghost" (91 times), "wind" (1 time). "life" (1 time), but never as "breath" or "breathed."

What he said may be true of the Greek word "pneuma" but guess what the root word of this is? That's right, "pneo." Plus, an honest look into the definition of pneo and pneuma will show you that the idea of blowing, or breathing is in both definitions. Here they are,

> "Pneo a primary word; to breathe hard, i.e. breeze: --blow." And now, "pneuma from pneo; a current of air, i.e. breath (blast) or a breeze; by analogy or figuratively, a spirit, i.e. (human) the rational soul, (by implication) vital principle, mental disposition, etc., or (superhuman) an angel, demon, or (divine) God, Christ's spirit, the Holy Spirit: --ghost, life, spirit (-ual, -ually), mind. "

I know there are some who do not like the source that I got that from so here is a different one from the internet.

> "The phrase, given by inspiration of God, is in one word in the Greek text. It is the word, theopneustos, which means, God breathed. It is a compound word, with theo the Greek word for God, attached to the word pneustos which means

CHAPTER 7: THE EFFICACY OF GOD'S WORD

wind, or spirit, or breath. We have this word in our English word pneumonia – a disease of the breath or lungs."

Don't agree with the Greek? Let's look at the Latin again for a moment. The Latin for the word inspiration says, "in, meaning in (that was deep), and spirare (notice the spelling), which means (hold onto your hat) to breathe and conveys the idea of motion, direction, or inclination into or to a place or thing." Oh well, what do I know, I am just an Evangelist!

The important point though goes back to my question, "What makes the Bible effective in our lives?" In this verse, using the Greek, which the English and the Latin agrees with, it says that GOD inspired all Scripture. Another verse I want to look at is found in 1 Peter 1:23 which says, "Being born again, not of corruptible seed, but of incorruptible, by the word of God, which liveth and abideth for ever."

The argument on this verse is whether the word "which" refers to the Word or to God. To understand this will show us whether it is the Word which liveth and abideth forever or if it is God which liveth and abideth forever. I think it is obvious but what is obvious to me might not be to others.

One reason I think this is because I have heard a well-known preacher say, "The word "which" **never** refers to God!" He was talking about Philippians 4:13 which states, "I can do all things through Christ **which** strengtheneth me."

Well, when someone makes a statement like that I like to look it up. So, I went home, turned on my old laptop with my Bible programs on it. I typed in the word "which" and found many verses which contradict what the preacher said. Here is just one of them.

Psalm 115:15

*"Ye are blessed of the LORD **which** made heaven and earth."*

The old saying, "Never say never" applies here I think. That and, "Let God be true and every man a liar." It is obvious that the word "which" here DOES refer to God and there are many other verses which proves the same thing. The preachers reasoning behind the statement he made was based on his personal interpretation, which was based on another man's interpretation, that it is **doing** things for God which strengthens us but that is not only not correct, it is also guilty of taking the verse out of its context. A simple study of the verses previous to verse 13 shows us that the Apostle was telling the Philippian Christians that he was able, with God's help, to be content in what so ever state he was in. Look at the verses.

Philippians 4:10-13

> "But I rejoiced in the Lord greatly, that now at the last your care of me hath flourished again; wherein ye were also careful, but ye lacked opportunity. Not that I speak in respect of want: for I have learned, in whatsoever state I am, therewith to be content. I know both how to be abased, and I know how to abound: every where and in all things I am instructed both to be full and to be hungry, both to abound and to suffer need. I can do all things through Christ which strengtheneth me."

Paul was saying, he could be abased and abound, he could be full and hungry because Christ would strengthen him. The interpretation by the preacher who made the comment totally ignores this context and emphasized that we are to do different things and the doing of things would strengthen us. This proves the rule that a text taken out of the context makes it a pretext! "Which," in Philippians 4:13 is not referring to the doing, but to Christ. So, the word "which" can and does often refer to God as found in Psalm 115:15.

CHAPTER 7: THE EFFICACY OF GOD'S WORD

Then, in 1 Peter 1:23 what is the word "which" referring to? We have seen that the word "which" can, and often does, refer to God. Let's look at the verse again in 1 Peter 1:23.

"Being born again, not of corruptible seed, but of incorruptible, by the word of God, which liveth and abideth for ever."

According to many different sources I have used to look up this verse, the word "which" can, in this case, refer to both the word and God but that it must of necessity refer to God more than to the Word. This can only be used to show how the Word of God is effective. I have said, "The Word without God is dead and cannot live while the Word with God lives because He lives." The efficacy, or effectiveness, of the Scripture depends on the life of God. The Word without God cannot live! The Bible is not a living Book without God!

In an old book I have which was written by Dr. James B. Walker, a Baptist, on the Doctrine of the Holy Spirit written in 1874, it says, **"Truth never gives life to the heart and conscience so that they are empowered to govern the will, unless there be a sense of God in it.** This fact is verified in all history, as well as in the experience of individual men. The sages of antiquity perceived and announced many moral truths of the highest value, some of them synonymous with those of the New Testament. But what care men for moral truth when it is uttered only by one whom they esteem as a fellow mortal equal with themselves…**All experience teaches that truth, separate from a sense of the authority of God, does not become life in man's moral nature. It has no efficacy to quicken the conscience or to purify the heart. There is no moral efficacy even in inspired truth, unless the soul recognizes in it the will and heart of God in regard to man."**

God makes the Scriptures effective because He liveth and abideth forever! In the 1970's there was a popular saying going around that God was dead. If that could happen, and it cannot, then the Word of God cannot be effective, it is not alive without God! This is why I said earlier that the word, "which," must of necessity refer to God more than to the Word. It is God who makes the Bible effective and as Rev. Walker above said so well, "There is no moral efficacy even in inspired truth, unless the soul recognizes in it the will and heart of God in regard to man."

What else, or Who else makes the Scriptures effective in the lives of Christians?

Jesus makes the Bible effective in our lives!

As of the writing of this material (in 2012) I have been saved for 38 years. For the whole 38 years I have heard people say the following. "There is the written Word and there is the Living Word." To that I say, Amen! What is it that makes up the written Word and Who is the Living Word? What is it that makes them necessary to each other and how do they relate to each other? The answer to these questions is very easy. First of all let me say, that there has always been a written Word.

1 Peter 1:25

"But the word of the Lord endureth for ever. And this is the word which by the gospel is preached unto you."

Isaiah 40:8

"The grass withereth, the flower fadeth: but the word of our God shall stand for ever."

Psalm 119:89

"LAMED. For ever, O LORD, thy word is settled in heaven."

From the Treasury of David by Charles Haddon Spurgeon we have the following,

CHAPTER 7: THE EFFICACY OF GOD'S WORD

"The strain is more joyful, for experience has given the sweet singer a comfortable knowledge of the word of the Lord, and this makes a glad theme. After tossing about on a sea of trouble the Psalmist here leaps to shore and stands upon a rock. **Jehovah's word is not fickle nor uncertain; it is settled, determined, fixed, sure, immovable. Man's teachings change so often that there is never time for them to be settled; but the Lord's word is from of old the same, and will remain unchanged eternally.** Some men are never happier than when they are unsettling everything and everybody; but God's mind is not with them. **The power and glory of heaven have confirmed each sentence which the mouth of the Lord has spoken, and so confirmed it that to all eternity it must stand the same, -- settled in heaven, where nothing can reach it.** In the former section David's soul fainted, but here the good man looks out of self and perceives that the Lord fainteth not, neither is weary, neither is there any failure in his word.

The verse takes the form of an ascription of praise: the faithfulness and immutability of God are fit themes for holy song, and when we are tired with gazing upon the shifting scene of this life, the thought of the immutable promise fills our mouth with singing. God's purposes, promises, and precepts are all settled in his own mind, and none of them shall be disturbed. Covenant settlements will not be removed, however unsettled the thoughts of men may become; let us therefore settle it in our minds that we abide in the faith of our Jehovah as long as we have any being."

Later he wrote the following on this verse.

> "If we look at God's word of promise, as it is in our unsettled hearts, we dream that it's as ready to waver as our hearts are; as the shadow of the sun and moon in the water seems to shake as much as the water doth which it shines upon. Yet for all this seeming shaking here below, the sun and moon go on a steadfast course in heaven. So the Psalmist tells us that however our hearts stagger at a promise through unbelief, nay, and our unbelief makes us believe that the promise often is shaken; yet God's word is settled, though not in our hearts, yet "in heaven"; yea, and there "for ever," as settled as heaven itself is; yea, more than so; for "heaven and earth may pass," but "not one jot or tittle of the law (and therefore of the gospel) shall fail"

It is interesting to note that Spurgeon never does write that the Bible, as we have it in the King James, is written in heaven and that it is there just like we have it here. Most recent writers say that the Bible is written in heaven and that Psalm 119:89 is referring to that, but Spurgeon simply writes that what God says, all of it (and He has said more than what is written in the Bible) is settled, immutable. Now before you get your hackles up, this also includes not only all that He has said in eternity past, but also what He has written. What is written in the Bible is also settled, immutable, unchangeable throughout all time and eternity.

He has given us the written Word so that we can know Him and what He expects of us. He has given us the Word of God so we can know how to come to Him by faith in Christ and so we can have the wisdom of God in our hands and hearts. Thank God He gave us the written Word! But not only do we have the written Word, but we also have the Living Word Who also makes the written Word effective in our lives. Just as important as it is to have the living God, as we saw earlier, it is

CHAPTER 7: THE EFFICACY OF GOD'S WORD

also vital that we have the Living Word, Jesus Christ! Not only does the living God make the Bible effective, but also the Living Word makes it effective. You again cannot have one without the other! Why do we call Jesus the Living Word?

John 1:1-5

> ***"In the beginning was the Word, and the Word was with God, and the Word was God. The same was in the beginning with God.*** *All things were made by him; and without him was not any thing made that was made. In him was life; and the life was the light of men. And the light shineth in darkness; and the darkness comprehended it not."*

John 1:9-14

> *"That was the true Light, which lighteth every man that cometh into the world. He was in the world, and the world was made by him, and the world knew him not. He came unto his own, and his own received him not. But as many as received him, to them gave he power to become the sons of God, even to them that believe on his name: Which were born, not of blood, nor of the will of the flesh, nor of the will of man, but of God.* ***And the Word was made flesh, and dwelt among us,*** *(and we beheld his glory, the glory as of the only begotten of the Father,) full of grace and truth."*

Revelation 19:13

> *"And he was clothed with a vesture dipped in blood: and his name is called* ***The Word of God.****"*

I have often said that you cannot be right with God and be wrong with the Word of God! You cannot be right with God and be wrong with the written or the Living Word! To be wrong with the written Word means that you are changing His Word and that you think that you know better than God. To be wrong with the

Living Word, Jesus, means that you are not only not right with God because peace with the Father comes only through the Son, but that you are also not right with the written Word which tells us how to have peace with God! Just like God the Father is always going to agree with His Word, God the Son is also always going to agree with the written Word! Jesus makes the Bible efficacious, or effective!

How important is it to be right with the written Word? How important is it to rightly divide the Scriptures? How important is it to be right with God? Crucially important! It makes the difference between heaven and hell and victory or defeat in our lives. To rightly divide the Word of truth means you come to knowledge of the Great Three in One, the Trinity of God!

Let me give you an example of how important it is to rightly divide the Word of Truth. There is a teaching lately that says that God has more of the written Word in heaven and that He chose from it all that we need and gave it to us in our Bible. They take this idea from John 21:25 which says,

> *"And there are also many other things which Jesus did, the which, if they should be written every one, I suppose that even the world itself could not contain the books that should be written. Amen."*

First of all that verse does not say what they are teaching but I will let the Bible speak for itself.

John 12:37

> *"But though he had done so many miracles before them, yet they believed not on him:"*

John 20:30

> *"And many other signs truly did Jesus in the presence of his disciples, **which are not written in this book:** But these are written, that ye might*

CHAPTER 7: THE EFFICACY OF GOD'S WORD

believe that Jesus is the Christ, the Son of God; and that believing ye might have life through his name."

John is simply saying, under inspiration of course, that not everything that Jesus did was written in this book (the book of John), but what was written was so they might believe that Jesus is the Christ. There were many things that Jesus did that were not necessary to write down for us, they were "...not written in this book..." and, according to John 21:25 above, if all Jesus did while on the earth had all been written down for us the world could not contain it all. To say that we do not have all the written Word of God but that there is more of it in heaven not only bends what John was inspired to write but it also implies that God has not given us all the Word of God! Well, there I go again, don't listen to me I am just an Evangelist! I am not trying to be controversial; I am trying to rightly divide the Word of truth. If rightly dividing the Bible makes me controversial, then so be it! I will answer to God Who inspired it and no man! We have all the Word of God; there is none of it waiting for us in heaven! The King James Bible has it all!

Since Jesus is the Living Word, then He also makes the Word of God effective in our lives. Because He lives, the Bible is not a dead Book! If He had stayed in the grave and not resurrected from the dead, then the Bible would not and could not be effective. But since He is the resurrected Saviour, then the Scriptures can be efficacious.

So, we have seen that God the Father and God the Son makes the Word of God effective. Want to venture a guess on Who else makes the Word of God effective?

The Holy Spirit makes the Word of God effective.

Probably the most famous verse talking about the Holy Spirits part in the giving of the Scriptures is found in 2 Peter 1:21 which says,

> *"For the prophecy came not in old time by the will of man: but holy men of God spake as they were moved by the Holy Ghost."*

Going back to a previous study, we see that the Holy Ghost also has a part of the giving of the Scriptures. But a thing I want you to notice, which I have not heard anyone talk about yet, is the part which says, "...holy men of God **spake** *as they were moved by the Holy Ghost.*" In my discussion about how God breathed the words of the Scriptures, I said that it is not wrong doctrinally to use the definition, "God breathed." It is not wrong and even gives a clear picture of how He gave us the words of Scripture...He breathed them, or He spoke them. In the verse above, we see that the holy men of God **SPAKE** as they were moved by the Holy Ghost. So, as the Holy Spirit moved the holy men of God, He caused them to speak. Speak what? To speak the words of the Word of God!

Another definition you must know is the definition on the word Spirit and Ghost in reference to the Holy Spirit. The Greek for Spirit is the word, "pneuma, " again, the root word "pneo" is a part of this but the definition of pneuma is...

> "a current of air, i.e. breath (blast) or a breeze; by analogy or figuratively, a spirit, i.e. (human) the rational soul, (by implication) vital principle, mental disposition, etc., or (superhuman) an angel, demon, or (divine) God, Christ's spirit, the Holy Spirit:"

So, it is not only acceptable to use the word breathed in our definition of the word inspiration, but it is also acceptable to use the word Spirit. They both come from the same Greek word and root word. It is ok, you can breathe now. The point I am making is that the Holy Spirit is a huge part of the inspiration of the Scriptures which makes Him another part of how the Bible is effective in our lives. Let me give you another set of verses.

CHAPTER 7: THE EFFICACY OF GOD'S WORD

1 Corinthians 2:9-14

> *"But as it is written, Eye hath not seen, nor ear heard, neither have entered into the heart of man, the things which God hath prepared for them that love him.* **But God hath revealed them unto us by his Spirit:** *for the Spirit searcheth all things, yea, the deep things of God. For what man knoweth the things of a man, save the spirit of man which is in him? even so the things of God knoweth no man, but the Spirit of God.* **Now we have received, not the spirit of the world, but the spirit which is of God; that we might know the things that are freely given to us of God.** *Which things also we* **speak***, not in the words which man's wisdom teacheth, but which the Holy Ghost teacheth; comparing spiritual things with spiritual.* **But the natural man receiveth not the things of the Spirit of God: for they are foolishness unto him: neither can he know them, because they are**

There is quite a lot of information in this set of verses but I will try to confine myself to making just a few observations.

First, it says, "…**But God hath revealed *them* unto us by his Spirit…**" This shows us the efficacy of the Spirit of God. He reveals things to us from the Word of God. Since He was a part of the inspiration process, and because He is a part of the Trinity of God, He knows the mind of God and can reveal things to us from the Word of God. This is also talking about the inspiration of Scriptures but it shows the effectiveness of the Holy Spirit with the Word of God.

The next thing to point out is the part which says,

> "*…. Now we have received, not the spirit of the world, but the spirit which is of God;* **that we might know the things that are freely given to us of God.**"

The reason we know the things of God is because we have the Spirit Who is behind all the Scriptures and always agrees with the Word of God. The point of this section is that not only are the Scriptures effective because of God the Father and God the Son, but they are effective because of God the Holy Spirit.

Now having said all of that, there are some other factors which determine whether or not the Scriptures are effective or not.

The Scriptures are effective if you are saved!

With all this having been said, even though the God of all creation is behind the Scriptures, in order for them to be truly effective in someone's life, a person must be a saved individual. The reason is found in this part of 1 Corinthians 2 which says,

> *"But the natural man receiveth not the things of the Spirit of God: for they are foolishness unto him: neither can he know them, because they are spiritually discerned."*

Because the Word of God is Spiritually given and discerned, then a person must be born of the Spirit in order for the Word of God to be effective. This is why Jesus said the following.

John 3:5 & 6

> *"Jesus answered, Verily, verily, I say unto thee, Except a man be born of water and of the **Spirit**, he cannot enter into the kingdom of God. That which is born of the flesh is flesh; and that which is **born of the Spirit is spirit**."*

An unsaved person does not have the Spirit of God and cannot understand the things of God because they are spiritually discerned. Why must a person be born again? A person must be born again because if they are not then the Scriptures cannot do their work in a person's life. The Scriptures tell us that a person who is not born again is dead in his trespasses and sins. (Ephesians 2:1) I have always asked the question, what can a

CHAPTER 7: THE EFFICACY OF GOD'S WORD

dead person understand? The answer is obvious, nothing! Therefore Jesus Himself said that a person who is dead because of his trespasses and sins, must be born again of the Spirit...THEN AND ONLY THEN CAN THE SCRIPTURES BE EFFECTIVE AND PRODUCE THE DESIRED EFFECTS! Not only must a person be born again in order for the Scriptures to be efficacious, but...

In order for the Scriptures to be effective we must be surrendered to God's will.

With just some natural common sense, even if a person is saved, that does not insure that the Scriptures will produce anything in a person's life. They must also be a surrendered person and have the attitude that whatever God says in His Word is truth, and then the saved person must be surrendered to it. If God says that we are not to commit adultery and we do not listen to Him in His Word and we refuse to listen to the Holy Spirit, then the Word is of no effect in our lives. When God says that we are to be witnesses to others about Christ and we do not listen and obey, then the promises are of no value to us because we are not surrendered to His Word.

One of the most familiar verses in the Bible about being surrendered to God's will is found in Romans 12:1 and 2 which says, "I beseech you therefore, brethren, by the mercies of God, that ye present your bodies a living sacrifice, holy, acceptable unto God, *which* is your reasonable service. And be not conformed to this world: but be ye transformed by the renewing of your mind, that ye may prove what *is* that good, and acceptable, and perfect, will of God."

We are to be surrendered people to God and His will as revealed in the Scriptures and any time we are not surrendered to His will, then the Scriptures are not effective. Another way for the Scriptures to be effective is as follows.

The Scriptures can be effective if we study them.

One verse in the Bible which is vital to our Christian growth is found in 2 Timothy 2:15.

"Study to shew thyself approved unto God, a workman that needeth not to be ashamed, rightly dividing the word of truth."

Think with me about this a moment. What would happen to a person who is saved and surrendered, but who does not KNOW what God says? This is where the Jews were when it says, "For I bear them record that they have a zeal of God, but not according to knowledge." (Romans 10:2) By the way, this also applies to any Christian who does not know the Scriptures. The Jews were possibly depending on their special status with God; they had a zeal for God but a zeal that was not based on knowledge. They knew Him but not His Word and will. How do we combat that in our lives? S-T-U-D-Y! Study! Study what? The Scriptures! It is wonderful to be saved and even more so when you are surrendered to His will. But we must KNOW His Word in order for it to be effective in our lives.

Are you saved? Are you surrendered? Are you studying? Is the Word of God efficacious, or effective, in your life? How effective is it? These are the questions that you need to ask yourself and be honest about. Only you know how effective the Scriptures are and only you can determine how effective they are in your life. I challenge you to Study to show yourself approved, being not ashamed and rightly dividing the Word of truth. Make the Scriptures as effective in your life as God wants them to be.

Chapter 8
Preserved and Continuous Inspiration?

According to a few people today, there is what they call "preserved inspiration" and "continuous inspiration." Those who teach this start out with the incorrect definition and understanding of the word inspiration again totally ignoring the Greek word theopneustos. Whenever you start out incorrectly, you have to keep inventing ways to justify your wrong definition and understanding. They believe that inspiration is simply God's breath IN the words of Scripture. They believe that the Bible actually breathes, as I saw one man constantly act out the process of breathing as he spoke about this. He even also taught that the Bible literally speaks and that it thinks making it alive. He would illustrate this by taking in large amounts of air into his lungs then exhaling saying this is what the Word of God does proving it is "preserved inspiration" and then calling it "continuous inspiration." He would then use Hebrews 4:12 b which says, "…and *is* a discerner of the thoughts and intents of the heart." He used the word "discerner" to teach his doctrine that the Bible **thinks.**

That verse does not teach that the Bible "thinks" and, as is always the case, is a new teaching which has never been taught by any of our predecessors. Its correct teaching is that the Word of God is a discerner or distinguishes or tells the difference of the thoughts and intents of the heart. The Spirit in our lives shows us, using Scripture, what is right and wrong and then is a discerner of our thoughts and intents of our hearts. In our hearts we might want to harm someone in some way but then when we read the Bible the Spirit convicts our hearts of the wickedness we intend by showing us in Scripture that we are sinning with evil thoughts. The Spirit of God in us shows us if our thoughts and intents of the heart are right or wrong. THAT is what this verse teaches, not that the Bible thinks!

In Webster's 1828 dictionary the definition for discern is, "That which distinguishes; or that which causes to understand." Therefore, when the Word of God is discerning, it is not thinking, it is telling us the difference between right and wrong and shows us whether the thoughts and intents of our hearts are right or wrong! IT DOES NOT THINK! IT DOES NOT INHALE AND EXHALE!

In the Geneva Bible translation notes it says, "An amplification taken from the nature of the word of God, so powerful that it enters even to the deepest and most inward and secret parts of the heart, fatally wounding the stubborn, and openly reviving the believers." And then with respect to Hebrews 4:12a which says, "For the word of God is quick, and powerful, and sharper than any two-edged sword,..." it explains its thus. "He calls the word of God living, because of the effect it has on those to whom it is preached." As I have said previously, the Spirit of God uses the words of the Word of God in our lives, it is not the breath of God IN the words, it is the Spirit of God in us Who uses the words of the Word of God to convict, instruct and correct us.

But what about the "proof texts" of John 6:63; Hebrews 4:12 and I Peter 1:23? Don't they tell us that the Word of God is alive? Not in the way some are teaching it. Is the Word of God alive? All of my Christian life I have heard it put this way, so please excuse me for repeating what I have always heard but I want to teach the SAME thing to the next generation. There is the living Word of God and His name is Jesus Christ, and there is the written Word of God which we call the Bible. When we say that the Constitution is a living document, what is meant is that it is still as relevant today as it was when it was written. the Bible is that way too. It is still as relevant today as it was when it was written.

CHAPTER 8: PRESERVED AND CONTINUOUS INSPIRIATION?

By the way, let me insert this little bit of information right here. I recently heard a man say that Satan has words he uses to replace words that God intended to use. He said that the word "Bible" is Satan's replacement for the word "scripture." I don't know where he heard that or if he came up with that on his own...but that is just heretical! As soon as I heard that my blood started boiling and I did not listen to the rest of his message. I was too busy looking up things in the BIBLE. What I found was interesting. Did God ever use the word Bible to refer to His Word?

The word "bible" is not found in the Bible in **English**, you have to go to the **Greek** to find it. But since this man, and many others, do not use that "old and dead" language (I am dripping with sarcasm) they then assume that since it is not found in the Bible in English then it must not be a word God would use. But, since the Hebrew, Aramaic and Greek are the languages God gave man the words of the Word of God in, then let's see if we can find the word "bible" in any of those "dead languages."

Mark 12:26 says,

*"And as touching the dead, that they rise: have ye not read in **the book** of Moses, how in the bush God spake unto him, saying, I am the God of Abraham, and the God of Isaac, and the God of Jacob?"*

The word "book" referring to the book of Moses in the Pentateuch in the Greek is the word, "BIBLOS!"

Luke 3:4 says,

*"As it is written in **the book** of the words of Esaias the prophet, saying, The voice of one crying in the wilderness, Prepare ye the way of the Lord, make his paths straight."*

Again the word "book" referring to the book of Esaias in the Greek is the word, "BIBLOS!" Do you begin to see a pattern here?

Luke 20:42 refers to the "book of Psalms." The book of John is referred to in John 20:30. Acts 7:42 refers to the book of the prophets. Hebrews 10:7 refers to the volume of the book it is written of me. John was told to write in a book and send it to the seven churches the things he saw on Patmos in Revelation 1:11. There are many other references (40 in total) where the English word book is used 47 times and the Greek word for the word book is the Greek word "BIBLOS!" Now, since GOD used the word BIBLOS referring to the all the Old Testament books of the Bible in the few verses I have above...is it really Satan's replacement word for Scripture as the preacher said. NO! NO! NO! A THOUSAND TIMES NO! The Holy Bible is the Holy Book because it has God as its author! God called the different books BIBLOS. It is not Satan's replacement for the word Scripture! I need to take another blood pressure pill! My point in this is we must not be afraid to use the Hebrew and Greek languages in our study of the BIBLE! And in our study of the "proof texts" referred to previously we also need to use correct Bible study principles to correctly understand what those verses are teaching.

John 6:63 says,

"It is the spirit that quickeneth; the flesh profiteth nothing: the words that I speak unto you, they are spirit, and they are life."

Jesus had been teaching about eat His flesh and drinking His blood in a spiritual sense as compared to a fleshly one. He was NOT talking about literally eating His flesh and drinking His blood. The people did not understand what He was teaching and it says in verse 60, "Many therefore of his disciples, when they had heard *this*, said, This is an hard saying; who can hear it?" They murmured at His teaching and because of their misunderstanding of it Jesus then explained in verse 63 as we see above. "It is the spirit that quickeneth; the flesh profiteth nothing: the words that I speak unto you, *they* are spirit, and *they* are life."

Again, John Gill says about this,

"...it is spiritual eating, or eating the flesh, and drinking the blood of Christ in a spiritual sense, which quickens, refreshes, and comforts the minds of believers; it is that by, and on which they live, and by which their spiritual strength is renewed:"

Jesus was not teaching that the words were alive, because it is the Spirit of God Who gives life after the Word of God is planted in the heart. Jesus was NOT teaching in John 6:63 that the words were alive, but that the Spiritual teaching of Jesus here is what GIVES us life. Again John Gill explains it this way,

"the words that I speak unto you, *they* are spirit, and *they* are life; the doctrines which Christ had then been delivering concerning himself, his flesh and blood, being spiritually understood, are the means of quickening souls. The Gospel, and the truths of it, which are the wholesome words of our Lord Jesus Christ, are the means of conveying the Spirit of God, as a spirit of illumination and sanctification, into the hearts of men, and of quickening sinners dead in trespasses and sins: the Gospel is the Spirit that giveth life, and is the savour of life unto life, when it comes not in word only, or in the bare ministry of it, but with the energy of the Holy Ghost, and the power of divine grace."

Adam Clarke's commentary on the Bible says,

"**Are spirit, and they are life** - As my words are to be spiritually understood, so the life they promise is of a spiritual nature:"

In Albert Barnes Notes on the New Testament he wrote,

"They are spirit. They are spiritual. They are not to be understood literally, as if you were really to eat my flesh, but they are to be understood as denoting the need of that provision for the soul which God has made by my coming into the world. (they) Are life. (It does not say that they are living, it says they are life!) Are fitted to produce or give life to the soul dead in sins."

No…this "proof text" does not teach that the Bible is actually alive and breathing. Again, as I have heard all my Christian life (40 plus years), and as Dr. Jack Hyles himself taught about this, "There are two "words of God," the Bible is the written word of God and Jesus is the living word of God!"

(www.baptist-city.com/sermons/god's_words.htmpage 3)

The incorrect teaching is that the breath of God abides in the words of the Bible which makes them alive. No! they are alive because God is alive and the Holy Spirit is Who quickens us as we learn from the Word of God of our need of Jesus for our Saviour. It is the Holy Spirit Who is the breath if you will and He indwells us not the Scriptures! 2 Corinthians 3:6 says, "Who also hath made us able ministers of the new testament; not of the letter, but of the spirit: for the letter killeth, but the spirit giveth life." Again, on this verse Gill writes, "**the spirit, which giveth life**; it is a means in the hand of the Spirit of God, of quickening dead sinners, of healing the deadly wounds of sin, of showing the way of life by Christ, and of working faith in the soul, to look to him, and live upon him; it affords food for the support of the spiritual life, and revives souls under the most drooping circumstances."

Another of their "proof texts" is Hebrews 4:12 which says, "For the word of God *is* quick, and powerful, and sharper than any twoedged sword, piercing even to the dividing asunder of soul and spirit, and of the joints and marrow, and *is* a discerner of the thoughts and intents of the heart." The word "quick" in here means, "to *live* (literally or figuratively): - life (-time), (a-) live (-ly), quick. (Strong's Concordance – G-2198)

I believe that the life of the Word of God depends on the life of God Himself and that this is what this verse is teaching. The Bible is alive and active, not because it has its own life source in its words, but because God is alive.

In the Family Bible Notes it says,

"The word of God; all his declarations, whether of law or grace, whether of promise or threatening. God, who is its author, imparts to it his own divine energy. It lays open every heart, and detects all hypocrisy and unbelief. Quick; living, and powerful in its effects. Joh 6:63; 2Co 10:4; Two-edged sword; Eph 6:17; Re 1:16; 19:15. Discerner of the thoughts; lays open the secrets of the heart, and shows a man to himself. Ro 7:7. Our faith, therefore, must be hearty, active, and persevering, or we shall fail of obtaining the promised rest. The word of God; all his declarations, whether of law or grace, whether of promise or threatening. God, who is its author, imparts to it his own divine energy. It lays open every heart, and detects all hypocrisy and unbelief. Quick; living, and powerful in its effects. Joh 6:63; 2Co 10:4; Two-edged sword; Eph 6:17; Re 1:16; 19:15. Discerner of the thoughts; lays open the secrets of the heart, and shows a man to himself. Ro 7:7. Our faith, therefore, must be hearty, active, and persevering, or we shall fail of obtaining the promised rest."

The phrase "word of God" is interchangeable with the Scriptures and with what God has said. For example, Hebrews 11:3 says, **"Through faith we understand that the worlds were framed by the word of God,** so that things which are seen were not made of things which do appear." We understand that the phrase "word of God" here means that God spoke the worlds into existence and not that the Scriptures or the Bible spoke them into existence. So, there are definite places in the Bible where the phrase "word of God" is not talking about the Scriptures but what God said as in this case.

Those who teach that Hebrews 4:12 teaches that the word of God (the Bible) is quick or alive, totally ignore that the life of the Bible is backed, if you will, by the life of God! If God is not alive, neither is the Bible! Since God is alive, so is the Bible, but not the way they teach where it actually breathes and thinks. I must add 1 Peter 1:23 here to help me with Hebrews 4:12.

1 Peter 1:23 says,

"Being born again, not of corruptible seed, but of incorruptible, by the word of God, **which** *liveth and abideth for ever."*

It was taught once in connection with Philippians 4:13 which says, "I can do all things through Christ which strengtheneth me." that the word **which** "NEVER refers to Christ" in this teachers effort to twist the teachings of the verse to make it mean it is the doing of things that strengthens us and not Christ Who strengthens us. After he made that comment, I went home to dig it out to see if what he said was true. Using my Bible program in my laptop, I punched in "the Lord which" and other combinations of words to see if "which" is EVER used in connection with God, Christ, Lord or any other name of God. It took me to a verse in Psalm 115:15 which reads, "Ye *are* blessed of the **LORD which** made heaven and earth." The word "which" here definitely refers to the Lord WHICH made heaven and earth! So, his statement was not true and neither was his

CHAPTER 8: PRESERVED AND CONTINUOUS INSPIRIATION?

teaching! Therefore, in 1 Peter 1:23 where it says, "…by the word of God WHICH liveth and abideth forever," I also come to the conclusion that the life of the Bible depends on the life of God! The word of God the Bible CANNOT liveth and abideth forever if GOD does not live and abide forever!

Richard Bancroft's rules for translation of the King James Bible in rule 14 says,

> "These translations to be used, when they agree better with the text than the Bishops Bible: Tyndale's, Matthews, Coverdale's, Whitchurches (Great), and the Geneva."

In the Geneva Bible, one of the translations they used in their work, in 1 Peter 1:23, it uses the word WHO instead of the word WHICH making the meaning then to be that it is God WHO liveth and abideth forever!

A very familiar verse talking about the word of God is found in Psalms 119:89 which reads,

> *"LAMED. For ever, O LORD, thy word is settled in heaven."*

What all is that verse speaking about? Is it talking about the word of God the Bible? Of course it is! It is also talking about things God said that are not found in the Bible. Verses 90 and 91 show us this when they say,

> *"Thy faithfulness is unto all generations: thou hast established the earth, and it abideth. They continue this day **according to thine ordinances:** for all are thy servants."*

In Spurgeon's Treasury of David he wrote,

> "The strain is more joyful, for experience has given the sweet singer a comfortable knowledge of the word of the Lord, and this makes a glad theme. After tossing about on a sea of trouble the

Psalmist here leaps to shore and stands upon a rock. Jehovah's word is not fickle nor uncertain; it is settled, determined, fixed, sure, immovable. Man's teachings change so often that there is never time for them to be settled; but the Lord's word is from of old the same, and will remain unchanged eternally. Some men are never happier than when they are unsettling everything and everybody; but God's mind is not with them. The power and glory of heaven have confirmed each sentence which the mouth of the Lord has spoken, and so confirmed it that to all eternity it must stand the same, -- settled in heaven, where nothing can reach it. In the former section David's soul fainted, but here the good man looks out of self and perceives that the Lord fainteth not, neither is weary, neither is there any failure in his word.

The verse takes the form of an ascription of praise: the faithfulness and immutability of God are fit themes for holy song, and when we are tired with gazing upon the shifting scene of this life, the thought of the immutable promise fills our mouth with singing. God's purposes, promises, and precepts are all settled in his own mind, and none of them shall be disturbed. Covenant settlements will not be removed, however unsettled the thoughts of men may become; let us therefore settle it in our minds that we abide in the faith of our Jehovah as long as we have any being.

Thy faithfulness is unto all generations. This is an additional glory: God is not affected by the lapse of ages; he is not only faithful to one man throughout his lifetime, but to his children's children after him, yea, and to all generations so long as they keep his covenant and remember his

CHAPTER 8: PRESERVED AND CONTINUOUS INSPIRIATION?

commandments to do them. The promises are ancient things, yet they are not worn out by centuries of use, for the divine faithfulness endureth for ever. He who succoured his servants thousands of years ago still shows himself strong on the behalf of all them that trust in him. "Thou hast established the earth, and it abideth." Nature is governed by fixed laws; the globe keeps its course by the divine command, and displays no erratic movements: the seasons observe their predestined order, the sea obeys the rule of ebb and flow, and all things else are marshalled in their appointed order. There is an analogy between the word of God and the works of God, and specially in this, that they are both of them constant, fixed, and unchangeable. God's word which established the world is the same as that which he has embodied in the Scriptures; by the word of the Lord were the heavens made, and specially by him who is emphatically THE WORD. When we see the world keeping its place and all its laws abiding the same, we have herein assurance that the Lord will be faithful to his covenant, and will not allow the faith of his people to be put to shame. If the earth abideth the spiritual creation will abide; if God's word suffices to establish the world surely it is enough for the establishment of the individual believer.

EXPLANATORY NOTES AND QUAINT SAYINGS.

Ver. 90. -- Thy faithfulness is unto all generations. As he gathered, the certainty of God's word from the endurance of heaven, so now he confirms it by considering the foundation of the earth. Since the foundation of the earth, made by the word of God, abides sure, shall we not think that the foundation of our salvation laid in Jesus Christ, is much more sure? Though the creatures cannot teach us the way of our salvation (for that we must learn by the word), yet do they confirm that which the word saith, "Thus saith the LORD, which giveth the sun for a light by day, and the ordinances of the moon and of the stars for a light by night, which divideth the sea when the waves thereof roar; the LORD of hosts is his name: If those ordinances depart from before me, saith the LORD, then the seed of Israel also shall cease from being a nation before me for ever:" Jer 31:40,36. As there Jeremy gathers the stability of the church from the stability of the creatures; so here David confirms the certainty of our salvation by the most certain and unchangeable course of creation; and both of them are amplified by Christ Jesus: "Heaven and earth may pass away, but one jot of God's word shall not fall to the ground." Let us therefore be strengthened in faith and give glory to God. -- William Cowper.

Ver. 90. -- Thou hast established the earth, and it abideth. Every time we set foot on the ground, we may remember the stability of God's promises, and it is also a confirmation of faith. Thus, --

1. The stability of the earth is the effect of God's word; this is the true pillar upon which the earth standeth; for he upholdeth all things by the word of his power; "For he spake, and it was done; he commanded, and it stood fast": Ps 33:9. Now, his word of power helpeth us to depend upon his word of promise.

2. Nothing appeareth whereon the globe of the earth should lean and rest: "He stretcheth out the north over the empty place, and hangeth the earth

upon nothing:" Job 26:7. Now, that this vast and ponderous body should lean upon the fluid air as upon a firm foundation, is matter of wonder; the question is put in the book of Job: "Whereupon are the foundations thereof fastened? or who laid the cornerstone thereof?" Job 38:6. Yet firm it is, though it hang as a ball in the air...Now, since his word beareth up such a weight, and all the church's weight, and our own burden leaneth on the promise of God, he can, by the power of his word, bear up all without visible means. Therefore his people may trust his providence; he is able to support them in any distresses, when no way of help appeareth.

3. The firmness and stability offereth itself to our thoughts. The earth abideth in the same seat and condition wherein God left it, as long as the present course and order of nature is to continue: Ps 104:5. God's truth is as immovable as the earth: Ps 117:2. Surely if the foundation of the earth abideth sure, the foundation of our salvation, laid by Jesus Christ, is much more sure.

4. The stability remains in the midst of changes: Ec 1:4. All things in the world are subject to many revolutions, but God's truth is one and the same.

5. In upholding the frame of the world, all those attributes are seen, which are a firm stay to a believer's heart, such as wisdom, power, and goodness. The covenant of grace is as sure as the covenant made after the deluge. We cannot look upon this earth without seeing therein a display of those same attributes which confirm our faith, in waiting upon God till his promises be fulfilled to us. --Condensed from T. Manton.

Ver. 90. -- It abideth. Creation is as the mother, and Providence the nurse which preserveth all the works of God. God is not like man; for man, when he hath made a work, cannot maintain it: he buildeth a ship, and cannot save it from shipwreck; he edifies a house, but cannot keep it from decay. It is otherwise with God; we daily see his conserving power, upholding his creatures; which should confirm us that he will not cast us off, nor suffer us to perish (since we are the works of his hands) if we so depend upon him, and give him glory as our Creator, Conserver, and Redeemer. --William Cowper.

They continue this day according to thine ordinances. Because the Lord has bid the universe abide, therefore it stands, and all its laws continue to operate with precision and power. Because the might of God is ever present to maintain them, therefore do all things continue. The word which spake all things into existence has supported them till now, and still supports them both in being and in well being. God's ordinance is the reason for the continued existence of creation. What important forces these ordinances are! "For all are thy servants." Created by thy word they obey that word, thus answering the purpose of their existence, and working out the design of their Creator. Both great things and small pay homage to the Lord. No atom escapes his rule, no world avoids his government. Shall we wish to be free of the Lord's sway and become lords unto ourselves? If we were so, we should be dreadful exceptions to a law which secures the well being of the universe. Rather while we read concerning all things else -- they continue and they serve, let us continue to serve, and to serve more perfectly as our lives are continued. By that word which is settled may we be settled; by that voice which establishes the earth may we be established; and by that command which all created things obey may we be made the servants of the Lord God Almighty.

EXPLANATORY NOTES AND QUAINT SAYINGS.

Ver. 91. -- They continue this day according to thine ordinances, etc. Which of the works of God are not pervaded by a beautiful order? Think of the succession of day and night. Think of the revolution of the seasons. Think of the stars as they walk in their majestic courses, -- one great law of harmony "binding the sweet influence of the Pleiades,...and guiding Arcturus with his sons": Job 38:31-32. Look upwards, amid the magnificence of might, to that crowded concave, -- worlds piled on worlds, -- and yet see the calm grandeur of that stately march; -- not a discordant note there to mar the harmony, though wheeling at an Inconceivable velocity in their intricate and devious orbits! These heavenly sentinels all keep their appointed watch towers. These Levites in the upper firmament, light their altar fires "at the time of the evening incense," and quench them again, when the sun, who is appointed to rule the day, walks forth from his chamber. "These wait all upon thee": Ps 104:27. "They continue this day according to thine ordinances: for all are thy servants." --J.R. Macduff, in "Sunsets on the Hebrew Mountains," 1862.

Ver. 91. -- They continue this day according to thine ordinances. Man may destroy a plant, but he is powerless to force it into disobedience to the laws given it by the common Creator. "If," says one, "man would employ it for his use, he must carefully pay attention to its wants and ways, and bow his own proud will to the humblest grass at his feet. Man may forcibly obstruct the path of a growing twig, but it turns quietly aside, and moves patiently and irresistibly on its appointed way.". Do what he may, turf wilt not grow in tile tropics, nor the palm bear its fruit in a cold climate. Rice refuses to thrive out of watery swamps, or cotton to form its fleece of snowy fibres where the rain can reach them. Some of the handsomest flowers in the world, and stranger still, some of the most juicy and succulent plants with which we are acquainted, adorn the arid and desolate sands of the Cape of Good Hope, and wilt not flourish elsewhere. If you twist the branch of a tree so as to turn the under surface of its leaves towards the sky, in a very little while all those leaves will turn down and assume their appointed position. This process will be performed sooner or later, according to the heat of the sun and the flexibility of the leaves, but none the less it will surely take place. You cannot induce the Sorrowful tree of India to bloom by day, or cause it to cease all the year round from loading the night air with the rich perfume of its orange like flowers. The philosopher need not go far to find the secret of this. The Psalmist declares it when, speaking of universal nature, he traces the true cause of its immutable order. God, he says, "hath established them for ever and ever: He hath made a decree which shall not pass;" or, as it is in the Prayer book version, "hath given them a law which shall not be broken": Ps 148:6. Truly is it said in another Ps 114:8, "They continue this day according to thine ordinances: for all are thy servants." Wilful man may dare to defy his Maker, and set at nought his wise and merciful commands; but not so all nature besides. Well, indeed, is it for us that his other works have not erred after the pattern of our rebellion; that seed time and harvest, cold and heat, summer and winter, day and night, with all their accompanying provision, have not ceased! To the precepts imposed upon vegetation when first called into being on creation's third day, it stilt yields implicit submission, and the most tender plant will die rather than transgress. What an awful

CHAPTER 8: PRESERVED AND CONTINUOUS INSPIRIATION?

contrast to this is the conduct of man, God's noblest work, endowed with reason and a never dying soul, yet too often ruining his health, wasting and destroying his mental power, defiling his immortal spirit, and, in a word, madly endeavouring to frustrate every purpose for which he was framed. --James Neil, in "Rays from the Realms of Nature," 1879.

> Ver. 91. -- All creatures punctually observe the law he hath implanted on their nature, and in their several capacities acknowledge him their sovereign; they move according to the inclinations he imprinted on them. The sea contains itself in its bounds, and the sun steps not out of his sphere; the stars march in their order: "They continue this day according to thine ordinances: for all are thy servants." If he orders things contrary to their primitive nature they obey him. When he speaks the word, the devouring fire becomes gentle, and toucheth not the hair of the children he will preserve; the hunger starved lions suspend their ravenous nature when so good a morsel as Daniel is set before them; and the sun, which had been in perpetual motion since its creation, obeys the writ of ease God sent in Joshua's time, and stands still. --Stephen Charnock.
>
> Ver. 91. -- All are thy servants. We should consider how great is that perversity by which man only, formed in the image of God, together with reprobate angels, has fallen away from obedience to God; so that what is said of all other creatures cannot be said of him, unless renewed by singular grace. --Wolfgang Musculus."

You can tell that Spurgeon was a man who read many different areas of life from the quotes and things he made comparisons with. But as I read and re-read all this I came to the conclusion that our God is a great God, Who loves us and I am so very thankful that what He says will last throughout eternity! If there is anyone who keeps His word it is God and His word will not fail! The Word of God depends on the life of God!

In 2 Peter 3:5 it states, "For this they willingly are ignorant of, that by the word of God the heavens were of old, and the earth standing out of the water and in the water:" Again, when it says, "...by the word of God the heavens were of old..." is not talking about the Bible, but what God said in His creation of the heavens and the earth.

In the context of the verses starting in verse three of 2 Peter chapter three through verse seven is the following, "Knowing this first, that there shall come in the last days scoffers, walking after their own lusts, And saying, Where is the promise of his coming? for since the fathers fell asleep, all things continue as *they were* from the beginning of the creation. For this they willingly are ignorant of, that by the word of God the heavens were of old, and the earth standing out of the water and in the water: Whereby the world that then was, being overflowed with water, perished: But the heavens and the earth, which are now, by the same word are kept in store, reserved unto fire against the day of judgment and perdition of ungodly men." Knowing this first, that there shall come in the last days scoffers, walking after their own lusts, And saying, Where is the promise of his coming? for since the fathers fell asleep, all things continue as *they were* from the beginning of the creation. For this they willingly are ignorant of, that by the word of God the heavens were of old, and the earth standing out of the water and in the water: Whereby the world that then was, being overflowed with water, perished: But the heavens and the earth, which are now, by the same word are kept in store, reserved unto fire against the day of judgment and perdition of ungodly men.

The scoffers have one thing to say while God has another! The scoffers say, "Where is the promise of his coming? For since the

CHAPTER 8: PRESERVED AND CONTINUOUS INSPIRIATION?

fathers fell asleep, all things continue as they were from the beginning of creation." To which God replies, "For this they willingly are ignorant of, that **by the word of God the heavens were of old**, and the earth standing out of the water and in the water: Whereby the world that then was, being overflowed with water, perished: But the heavens and the earth, which are now, **by the same word are kept in store**, reserved unto fire against the day of judgment and perdition of ungodly men." The phrase, "by the word of God the heavens were of old..." and, "by the same word," is not simply referring to the Scriptures, though the Scriptures does include what God said at creation, but it refers to what God said, all that God said and intended for creation. This again agrees with Psalm 119:89 that things will happen and continue according to what God said because what He says IS SETTLED! IT WON'T CHANGE!

I believe that the life of the Word of God depends on the life of God and thank His Holy Name, He is eternal! Therefore, since the word "which" can and does refer to the Lord, or God, it can and does refer to God in 1 Peter 1:23 which again says,

> *"Being born again, not of corruptible seed, but of incorruptible, by the word of God, which liveth and abideth for ever."*

The Word liveth and abideth forever because God lives and abides forever! The life of the Word depends on the life of God!

Now I think I have taken care of the verses used to say that the Bible lives (breathes, thinks etc.). It does, in the Lord Jesus Who is the Living Word. (John 1:1, 2 and Revelation 19:13) It cannot be a living word outside of the life of the Trinity! If they were to die then the word of God would be dead too. Yes, the Word of God lives, but not like some who say that it literally breathes and thinks!

After having said all of that, what then about what is called preserved and continuous inspiration? These teachings begin with the wrong definition of inspiration. When you start out with a wrong definition you then start building a doctrine on a false premise. Let me give you an example. Within the past year there was a debate in our religious world about the word "eunuch." What is a eunuch? Well, if you go by the correct and predominantly accepted definition given in a dictionary, a eunuch is as follows taken from the Webster's 1828 Dictionary.

"**EU'NUCH**, n. [Gr. a bed, and to keep.] A male of the human species castrated.

From Strong's Concordance is the following,

G2135

εὐνοῦχος

eunouchos

yoo-noo'-khos

From εὐνή eune (a *bed*) and G2192; a *castrated person* (such being employed in Oriental bed chambers); by extension an *impotent* or *unmarried* man; by implication a *chamberlain* (*state officer*): - eunuch.

When I typed in the word eunuch on the internet the first definition said, "A man who has been castrated, especially in the past one employed to guard the women's living areas at an oriental court." So, the common understanding of what a eunuch was, it is a man who had been castrated and who worked for a kingdom to guard the women. In the case in Acts chapter 8, this eunuch also had the charge of all the Queens treasure. Had he started out guarding the women and then was promoted? We do not know, but we do know he was a eunuch, a man who had been castrated.

One person used the Bible verses which talk about eunuchs, of which there are only 7 in the whole Bible with 5 of those coming from Acts chapter eight, (the other 2 are found in

CHAPTER 8: PRESERVED AND CONTINUOUS INSPIRIATION?

Isaiah 56:3 and Jeremiah 52:25) and came up with the definition that an eunuch is simply a man who works for a king or queen. Well, in that case Joseph in Genesis was a eunuch, but he was a married man whose wife had children. Kind of hard to be a eunuch and have children! Because of this definition, they began teaching that someone who is a eunuch today could be a married man who just decided not to have children! A wrong definition brings wrong teaching.

As stated earlier, some teach that inspiration is simply God's breath in or on the words of the Bible again totally ignoring the word theopneustos and the Holy Spirits correct connection with the Scriptures. They teach then inspiration is what God did to the Scriptures not how God GAVE the Scriptures. What does 2 Timothy 3:16a say? **"All scripture *is* given by inspiration of God,..."** I have a tendency to want to believe what the verses say, not a man's interpretation of them, especially when their definitions are wrong and they go against what the men of the past have taught us concerning the Scripture. Again, I want to teach the SAME things to faithful men who will then pass down to others what was passed down to us. This verse is not telling us what God did to the Scriptures, but how God gave us the Bible!

In John R. Rice's book <u>Our God Breathed Book – The Bible</u> (I am sure some will correct Dr. Rice in heaven when they see him about using the word "Bible" and his title about it being God breathed. I am dripping with sarcasm here.) On page 50 is a quote from Edward J. Young which says,

> "The word which for our purpose is of supreme importance is the word theopneustos, translated in the English Bible, "inspired of God." It is a compound, consisting of the elements **theo** (God) and **pneustos** (breathed). Now it is well to note that the word ends in the three letters tos! In the Greek language, words which 1) end in tos and 2) are compound with theo (God) are generally

PASSIVE in meaning….and we properly translate "breathed of God." This point is often overlooked and there have been those who have somewhat vigorously insisted that the meaning is active. They would therefore translate by the phrase, "breathing of God," in the sense that the Scriptures breathed forth or were IMBUED WITH THE SPIRIT OF GOD. The true meaning is PASSIVE (not active), "that which is breathed out by God…" He went on to say on page 51, "According to Paul, the Scriptures are not writings into which something Divine has been breathed; they are not even writings which are imbued with the Divine Spirit (at least this is not his emphasis in this passage). The Scriptures, Paul vigorously assert, are writings which came into being because they were **BREATHED OUT BY GOD HIMSELF!**"

A.R. Fausset wrote,

"What it (inspiration) says of Scripture is, not that it is "breathed into by God," or is the product of the Divine "in breathing" into its human authors, but that it is "breathed out by God." God breathed, the PRODUCT of the creative breath of God."

In Dr. Rice's book also on page 51 is this quote by Dr. Rice about Benjamin B. Warfield.

" Benjamin B. Warfield , tremendous scholar that he was, has a long chapter of 52 pages about God-Inspired Scripture" dealing with the Greek term used in 2 Timothy 3:16, THEOPNEUSTOS, quoting many scholars, repelling critics, he says, "For surely there was not conception more deeply rooted in the Hebrew mind, at least, than that of the creative breath of God…" and he infer that

CHAPTER 8: PRESERVED AND CONTINUOUS INSPIRIATION?

when God breathed out the Scripture, it was the same kind of perfect creative act as when He created the world of when He created man…he sums up his conclusion thus: "what is Theopneustos is God breathed produced by the active breath of the Almighty."

Notice when Fausset said that the Scripture is the PRODUCT of the creative breath of God, what he was saying is inspiration is not what God did to the Scriptures but how God GAVE the Scriptures! The Bible is the product of Gods breathing out the words of the Bible.

Also, when Young said that the Bible is not imbued with the Spirit and that inspiration does not mean that it was, the word imbued means, "to be infused, ingrained, saturated or permeated." Hence, the Scriptures are not infused, ingrained, saturated or permeated by the Spirit of God. PLEASE REMEMBER, HOLY MEN OF OLD SPAKE AS THEY WERE MOVED BY THE SPIRIT OF GOD, and that WE ARE INDWELT BY THE HOLY SPIRIT MAKING IT POSSIBLE FOR US TO UNDERTAND THIS SPIRITUALLY DISCERNED BOOK! But nowhere does the Bible teach that the Scriptures are imbued with the Spirit! He USES the words of Scripture to accomplish what needs to be accomplished and what needs to be taught.

The "preserved and continuous inspiration" teaching is that the BREATH of God in or upon the words is what is preserved or continues. This teaching then is that the Bible is inspired today, not because the words have been miraculously preserved, but because the breath of God is preserved or continues in the words. This then explains their reasoning behind the statement, "Preservation without inspiration (God's breath in the Scriptures) is a corpse without breath!" Their preservation, again, is not the preservation of the WORDS of the Word of God; it is the preservation of the breath of the Word of God. Again, this totally ignores the Holy Spirits connection with the Word of

God and it is NOT what Scripture teaches! ALL SCRIPTURE IS GIVEN (HOW?) BY GOD! GOD BREATHED (PASSIVE) ALL SCRIPTURE!

If the word theopneustos were in the active tense, then the translation of it would possibly say, All scripture is being given by inspiration of God. Those who do not understand that the word is not active but passive would argue that instead of saying God breathed, it would say God is breathing and it continues to breathe. The correct understanding of the "tos" at the end of theopneustos makes a huge difference. Passive means it is done or has been done, God breathed! Active would say God is breathing. Greek endings are crucial to translation and the men of Hampton Court understood that and correctly kept the translation, "All scripture is given by inspiration of God."

There is some debate about Psalm 12, which I will not wade into, but verses 6 and 7 says, "The words of the LORD *are* pure words: *as* silver tried in a furnace of earth, purified seven times. Thou shalt keep them, O LORD, thou shalt preserve them from this generation for ever."

What does the word "them" refer to in verse 7? "Thou shalt keep them…" The word "them" in verse 7 is referring to the word, "words" in verse 6." The promise of God is that He would keep, not the breath, but He would keep the WORDS! What He promised to preserve are the words that He spoke which are given by inspiration. The WORDS were given by inspiration and the WORDS are kept by preservation.

Let's look at some verses which speak about the way God gives the words.

1 Kings 12:22

"But the word of God came unto Shemaiah the man of God, saying,"

CHAPTER 8: PRESERVED AND CONTINUOUS INSPIRIATION?

Psalm 68:11

> *"The Lord gave the word: great was the company of those that published it."*

Psalm 119:88

> *"Quicken me after thy lovingkindness;* **so shall I keep the testimony of thy mouth."**

Psalm 138:4

> *"All the kings of the earth shall praise thee, O LORD,* **when they hear the words of thy mouth."**

Even in connection with creation it puts the breath of God in how He created things.

Psalm 33:6

> *"By the word of the LORD were the heavens made; and all the host of them* **by the breath of his mouth."**

David said in 2 Samuel 23:2, "The Spirit of the LORD spake by me, and his word *was* in my tongue," showing us very clearly the process by which God has spoken to us and given us His word. The breath of God is connected to SPEAKING the words of Scripture, not putting His breath into them!

Finally and quickly because it is a ridiculous teaching, is the teaching about continuous inspiration. This again is in connection with the wrong definition of inspiration. I personally heard this taught and almost laughed out loud, but I was too upset at it to do so. To "prove" **continuous inspiration** the preacher used Psalm 119:89-91 which I have dealt with already but want to show you how desperate some are to prove their new doctrine. Again, the verses say, "Psalm 119:89

> *LAMED. For ever, O LORD, thy word is settled in heaven. (90) Thy faithfulness is unto all generations: thou hast established the earth, and it*

*abideth. (91) They **continue** this day according to thine ordinances: for all are thy servants."*

The teaching went this way. Since the Word of God is settled forever in heaven, it then CONTINUES today. He lifted the word "continue" out of verse 91 to refer to "thy word" in verse 89 and used it to prove his doctrine of "continuous inspiration" to teach that the breath of God "continues," in the words. But the correct teaching from these verses is, they, the earth and all generations continue this day ACCORDING TO THINE ORDINANCES! Why? Because the Word of the Lord, what He says, is settled! A text taken out of its context always makes it a pretext and an incorrect definition and teaching of a word leads to more false teaching.

No! Emphatically, no, preserved and continuous inspiration are not Biblical. By the way, one of the proponents of these teachings has CHANGED his teaching through the years. This is not just an opinion of mine, I have his emails proving that at one time he taught the same things as we had been taught by our teachers, that inspiration meant God breathed and that the preservation was toward the words, not the breath. In a private conversation recently I was even told that his "new doctrines" are a direct result of his personal agenda against another preacher. I will stick with those before me who taught that inspiration was how God gave the Scriptures, not what He did to them! I refuse to change what has been taught to me because of the teachings of people who have been divorced and re married two or three times and I refuse to base my teaching on a woman's incorrect teaching regardless how popular she is! I will stick with preachers of the past who believed in verbal inspiration, who did great things for God in their lives and the holy men of old. I will preach and teach the same things!

Chapter 9

Willingly Ignorant?

2 Peter 3:3-7

> *"Knowing this first, that there shall come in the last days scoffers, walking after their own lusts,*
>
> *And saying, Where is the promise of his coming? for since the fathers fell asleep, all things continue as they were from the beginning of the creation.*
>
> ***For this they willingly are ignorant of****, that by the word of God the heavens were of old, and the earth standing out of the water and in the water:*
>
> *Whereby the world that then was, being overflowed with water, perished:*
>
> *But the heavens and the earth, which are now, by the same word are kept in store, reserved unto fire against the day of judgment and perdition of ungodly men."*

It is hard for me to understand why the scoffers mentioned in the verses above are "willingly ignorant." Why would someone be willingly ignorant? Why willingly ignore anything that is true, factual, easily proveable and accurate? What benefit is there for anyone to be willingly ignorant? In the case above a person has to be openly against God and what He said. I do not think that is the case with the people who teach that inspiration is not how God gave the Scriptures, but what God did to them. They do not refuse to believe in the God of the Bible as in the verses above, they simply have gone down a road without looking at all the evidence and trusting what God has said and how He said it. Theponeustos is not what God did to the Scriptures, it is how God gave the Scriptures. He gave them by His breath; He spoke them! I know many of the men who believe the incorrect definition and who teach the incorrect doctrine about inspiration, they are good men, but, for some reason have decided to ignore the true, factual, easily proveable and accurate definition and teaching about inspiration.

Some of them used to teach it correctly and their church doctrinal statement agreed with the correct definition and teaching about inspiration, but they have changed! Some have done so, I believe, out of trying to distance themselves from someone they did not like or agree with. They have taken their "stand" and the pendulum has gone as far the other way incorrectly as the pendulum went the other way for the one they were trying to distance themselves from. They are good men, but have swallowed the poison of incorrect definition and incorrect teachings. They have for one reason or another become willingly ignorant, they have chosen to willingly ignore what they were taught and what they themselves have taught in the past. The problem with this is that there are always other good men who, without digging into things themselves to see if those things are so, are then swayed to believe wrong teachings because a well-known preacher, or some who think they are well-known, said so! It should not matter what anyone says regardless of their standing in Christianity, what matters is what the Bible says and what others have said in agreement with the Bible. When men become followers of men, they then become a candidate for the "willingly ignorant" society.

Act 17:11 says about the people of Berea after they heard the preaching of Paul about the resurrection,

> *"These were more noble than those in Thessalonica, in that they received the word with all readiness of mind, and searched the scriptures daily, whether those things were so."*

They checked out what Paul taught with the Scriptures to see if what he taught was correct. They decided to be proactive in

CHAPTER 9: WILLINGLY IGNORANT?

their Christianity and searched out the Scriptures and in doing so they were more noble than those in Thessalonica!

Paul in his message to the Corinthian Christians wrote in 1 Corinthians 3:1-7, "And I, brethren, could not speak unto you as unto spiritual, but as unto carnal, *even* as unto babes in Christ. I have fed you with milk, and not with meat: for hitherto ye were not able *to bear it,* neither yet now are ye able. For ye are yet carnal: for whereas *there is* among you envying, and strife, and divisions, are ye not carnal, and walk as men? For while one saith, I am of Paul; and another, I *am* of Apollos; are ye not carnal? Who then is Paul, and who *is* Apollos, but ministers by whom ye believed, even as the Lord gave to every man? I have planted, Apollos watered; but God gave the increase. So then neither is he that planteth any thing, neither he that watereth; but God that giveth the increase." It does not matter what men say, it does not matter what I say, what does God say and those who have correctly repeated what God said. I base my whole belief on this topic of inspiration on what God said in 2 Timothy 3:16 where it says, "All scripture *is **given*** (how?) by inspiration of God," and then what men have taught that agrees with what God said! I am not going to simply be a follower of a man, or, in this case, the teachings of a woman who followed and parroted the teaching of a man. I choose not to be willingly ignorant, I choose to study out the facts of Scripture and history.

I have already included quotes from sources on what inspiration is. Quite simply, inspiration is how God originally gave all Scripture which is by His breath in speaking them to holy men of old.

We believe in what is called "verbal inspiration" which means that, "inspiration extends to the very words themselves. (From his article entitled, What Inspiration Is Not, on page 6 by Dr. David Brown President of the King James Bible Research Council). Isaiah 59:21 says,

"As for me, this *is* my covenant with them, saith the LORD; My spirit that *is* upon thee, and my words which I have put in thy mouth, shall not depart out of thy mouth, nor out of the mouth of thy seed, nor out of the mouth of thy seed's seed, saith the LORD, from henceforth and for ever."

God spoke the words of the Word of God to the writers of the originals. As we will see in the sections on preservation and translation, we have the Words of God given by inspiration, meticulously preserved by the Holy Spirit, and then, carefully, accurately, and faithfully translated in the King James Bible.

In Dr. Rice's book <u>Our God Breathed Book – The Bible</u> on page 241, he wrote,

"…what the Bible teaches is WORD inspiration, that is, that God gave the words in which the original Scriptures were written down. That is called verbal inspiration from the Latin word VERBUM, meaning word. So we say a man is "verbose" if he uses many words. The inspiration is verbal, that is, it is an inspiration of the words in the original manuscripts."

Now, before you go off the deep end and say that he teaches that the King James Bible is not God's word, that is not what he is teaching. The King James Bible is the perfectly, preserved Word of God in the English language by preservation and accurate translation. More will be said about that later.

In the same book on page 59 is a quote from Charles H. Spurgeon. A part of it says, "This volume (the Bible) is the writing of the living God: each letter was penned with an Almighty finger; each word in it dropped from the everlasting lips; each sentence was dictated by the Holy Spirit." This is verbal inspiration!

CHAPTER 9: WILLINGLY IGNORANT?

To ignore the correct definition of inspiration is to ignore all the evidence of the past and verbal inspiration and what it means. In doing my research through the years on this word I used many sources from many different ages and backgrounds. ALL of them but one said the same thing; inspiration means God breathed! The only source I have that disputes this comes from a preacher who is in the crowd which believes the wrong definition for inspiration. He even uses the wrong method for getting his definition. This crowd also teaches against using the Greek and Hebrew or any concordances and lexicons. In order to believe the wrong definition, you need to totally ignore the etymology and history of the word AND you must totally ignore the Greek definition, which the critics of the Greek and Hebrew say is corrected by the English. You have to totally ignore the gorilla in the room, you have to totally ignore what the Scriptures say, the historical understanding and teaching about the Greek word theopneustos and the word inspiration. You have to totally disregard the "tos" at the end of the Greek word theopneustos and what it means and you just in general ignore all the preachers, professors and scholars of the present and the past. Let's look again at what some have written about the word inspiration and the Greek word theopneustos.

Historically

In Lockyer's series of books from <u>All the Doctrines of the Bible</u> he wrote,

> "The particular word used by Paul (referencing the word Theopneustos) means God breathed."

In J. Vernon McGee's book <u>Thru the Bible</u>, volume 5 page 473 he wrote, "the word inspiration means God breathed."

Dr. Pierson said, "This (Bible) is a God breathed inspiration."

A.R. Fausset wrote, "It is breathed out by God."

He also wrote,

> "...the meaning of the original Greek, theopneustos...is literally God breathed. All Scripture is God breathed, that is, the Scripture is breathed out by God."

Shelton Smith, editor of the Sword of the Lord paper, in his pamphlet "<u>The Book We Call the Bible</u> wrote on page 7,

> "All Scripture means that from Genesis to Revelation – the entire Bible, cover-to-cover – all...is given by inspiration of God. Every detail of every chapter, from the "hereshith" (Hebrew for In the beginning) at the top of Genesis 1 to the Amen at the end of Revelation, is given to us directly from God. The word for inspiration in the Greek text is theopneustos. **It means God breathed**. Now that simply means the actual words of Scripture are the fruit of His very own breath. Pneustos in English is pneumatic, meaning, acting by compressed air. Its Hebrew counterpart is naphach (wind, air breathe). In this context of creating Scripture, it doesn't just mean that God exuded His influence upon it but **it means that He breathed out His words. The idea is that His words were constructed from His own mouth. He gave each of the writers His very own words**."

Dr. H.D. Williams in his book <u>The Miracle of Inspiration</u> wrote,

> "Inspiration is the miracle whereby the words of Scripture in Hebrew, Aramaic and Greek were God breathed and "once delivered" using "holy men of God" and their vocabulary, who perfectly recorded them "once" as they were "moved" along by the Holy Spirit in such a way that "all" the

CHAPTER 9: WILLINGLY IGNORANT?

words written are infallible and inerrant in the sixty-six books of the canon of Scripture."

Dr. David Sorensen who is on the board of the King James Bible Research Council and the author of many books on the Bible plus a commentary on the whole Bible wrote,

> "Any student of Scripture knows that (theoponeustos) means, God breathed. But what does God breathed mean? I submit that God breathed is a reference to being God spoken...Hundreds of times in the Bible, we read Thus saith the Lord. The Bible therefore is a God spoken book. Inspiration in its simplest sense is a figure of speech referring to how the Bible has come from the mouth of God"

Dr. Phil Stringer also a board member of the King James Research Council and author writes,

> "Inspiration took place when God took control of a person and spoke His words through them or caused them to write down His words."

Does any of this sound anything like Matthew 4:4 which says,

> *"But he answered and said, It is written, Man shall not live by bread alone, but by **every word that proceedeth out of the mouth of God**."*

Micky Carter in his book Things that are Different are not the Same wrote on page 17,

> "...inspired equals God breathed...Word for word, the very minute details (jots and tittles) were God breathed into man."

Dr. Sorenson again in his book God's Perfect Book :Duluth, Minn.: Northstar Ministries 2009,

" It is significant to note that it is the SCRIPTURES which are inspired…What they wrote were words – the basic vehicle of thought created by God Himself…the Bible is a God spoken book."

In the July/August 2008 issue of the <u>Baptist Magazine</u> Shelton Smith editor of the <u>Sword of the Lord</u> is quoted as writing, "When we say it (the Bible) was given by inspiration of God, we mean that God Himself gave us His own words." (Page 23)

Inspiration is not what God did TO the Scriptures but how He GAVE THEM! They were given by inspiration, by His breath, He spoke the words to holy men of old who spoke and wrote them. The King James Bible is God's inspired Word perfectly preserved through accurate translation and is the Word of God in English. A lot more will be said about preservation in the next section. Stay tuned! But let us not be willingly ignorant of truth, hard facts, and accurate statements. Let us be willingly studious, and even scholarly (a word and concept many run from) in our work on the Scriptures. We are supposed to, "Study to shew thyself approved unto God, a workman that needeth not to be ashamed, rightly dividing the word of truth. As I have said hundreds of times, If study causes us to rightly divide the word of truth then a lack of study will cause us to wrongly divide the word of truth! We are to be scholars in the Word of God. A scholar is simply "One who learns of a teacher; one who is under the tuition of a preceptor; a pupil; a disciple" (From Webster's 1828 dictionary) It also means more than that but a scholar is simply a student in its basic form. This is why, I believe, we should not ignore the writings of other men on a subject. What did those before us teach on inspiration? What is the consensus among those who were before us? If, after you study out a thing, the teaching goes against the Scriptures, then ignore their writings. But, if on the other hand, their writings agree with the Greek, Hebrew, history, etymology and facts, then do not be

CHAPTER 9: WILLINGLY IGNORANT?

willingly ignorant. I am fearful many, especially those who are teaching the wrong definitions about inspiration, have turned from and totally ignore the men of the past, and, in some cases, even their own mentors and preachers who taught them the correct way. Don't be a casualty by being willingly ignorant......*study!*

Chapter 10
What About Dual and Triple Inspiration?

Depending on your view or understanding of inspiration, you might or might not believe in what is called "dual" or "triple" inspiration. If you believe, as I do, that inspiration is simply how God gave the Word of God to Moses through John, then you do not believe in dual or triple inspiration. And, you will be in good company as you will see by the quotes. But, if you believe that inspiration means that God's breath is in the Scriptures, that inspiration is not how God gave the Scriptures but what He did to them, then you will believe in dual and triple inspiration. If you believe that inspiration is what God did to the Scriptures then you will believe that the translators of the King James Bible and other translations, were just as inspired as Moses through John and you will then believe in dual inspiration.

The problem with this again starts with the incorrect understanding of what inspiration is. This then leads to another huge problem and that is dual inspiration. Dual inspiration is most commonly connected with the King James Bible and means that men of Hampton Court, the translators of the King James Bible, were as inspired as the recorders of Scripture, Moses through John. In other words, just like God told Moses and all the other writers of Scripture (the holy men of old) exactly what to write, God also told the translators of the King James Bible the very words in the English language what to write. This would mean then that the men of Hampton Court, the translators, did not actually translate from the Hebrew and Greek into English, but that they were told directly by God what English words to write. We therefore have the first inspiration to Moses and the others and then we have the second inspiration to the men of Hampton Court, hence, dual inspiration.

CHAPTER 10: WHAT ABOUT DUAL AND TRIPLE INSPIRATION?

Triple inspiration teaching comes in where Jesus quoted Old Testament verses in the New Testament which I will not spend much time on because this is usually not taught by very many people even now. I will say this about triple inspiration, it is just as incorrect as dual inspiration. What Matthew through John wrote concerning what Jesus quoted from the Old Testament is not triple inspiration, it was given by inspiration to Matthew through John in the Greek language and simply included Jesus quotes from the Old Testament. Wherever a quote from Jesus from the Old Testament is in the New Testament is recorded, it was given to the writers of the New Testament by the Holy Spirit just like He told Moses through Malachi what to write in the Old Testament.

A main problem with those who teach dual inspiration is their total ignoring of the process of preservation and their incorrect basis for dual inspiration. Another problem is there has been many, many other languages that the Word of God has been translated into since early Christianity. Were all those also done by inspiration? The only one the proponents of dual inspiration talk about is the King James Bible, they never mention the other languages that the Word of God is in. Never!

In the letter to the reader from the men of Hampton Court is the following...

> "...for the behoof and the edifying of the unlearned which hungered and thirsted after righteousness, and had souls to be saved as well as they, insomuch that most nations under heaven did shortly after their conversion hear Christ speaking unto them in their mother tongue, not by the voice of their minister only, but also **by the written word translated...**"

Notice they did not say that the word which was written in the mother tongue was inspired, but that it was TRANSLATED! But, my point being there have been many,

many translations from the original languages (Hebrew, Aramaic and Greek). After the above statement by the translators of the King James Bible, they gave an extensive list of the languages the Word of God had been translated into. Were those Bibles all inspired like the originals were, being God-breathed as God told Moses through John exactly what words to write? Or, was the process of careful translation used to translate from the original languages into the receptor language thus giving that people of those different languages the Word of God in their language. The men of Hampton Court, the translators of the King James Bible, did not call them inspired, they said they were translated. Much more will be said about this in the section dealing with translation. My theory about why they mistakenly speak about the men of Hampton Court being inspired like the writers of Genesis through Revelation, and they do not mention anything about any other Bible in other languages, is because first of all they cannot read the other languages and secondly they think that only the King James Bible was inspired and that all others should of necessity come directly from the King James Bible. They teach that all Bibles in other languages should be translated not from the Hebrew, Aramaic and Greek but from the English in the King James Bible because "since the King James Bible is a product of dual inspiration, then the English corrects the Hebrew, Aramaic and Greek!" I guess those poor people before the King James Bible never did have the words of the Word of God and that God was wrong as He gave the Word of God to all the writers of the Old and New Testaments in Hebrew, Aramaic and Greek. I guess no one before 1611 had God's Word according to the dual inspiration people who believe in this and that the English corrects the Greek! Ridiculous and heretical!

The incorrect basis for dual and triple inspiration comes from their teaching that, since Jesus quoted Old Testament verses in the Greek, that proves that translators are inspired! This proves nothing of the sort! If I know another language and I am speaking to a person of that language and I quote John 3:16 to them in their language, am I being inspired? Or could it be that I am simply

CHAPTER 10: WHAT ABOUT DUAL AND TRIPLE INSPIRATION?

speaking in a language the person can understand? I think the latter is what is happening.

The men of Hampton Court in their letter to the reader wrote,

> "...Now what can be more available thereto, than to deliver God's book unto God's people in a tongue which they understand."

What is important to God is the speaking to people in their language, so, when Jesus quoted Old Testament verses in Greek, He was not proving that translations are inspired, He was simply speaking to them in their own language so they could understand what the Scriptures teach.

"Well," you say, "What Jesus quoted ended up in the Bible which is inspired so it does prove dual inspiration or even triple inspiration." It is nothing of the kind. What Jesus said in the Greek was simply an account of the conversation with whoever He was speaking to and it was recorded by inspiration for us to read and to be taught by.

It is much like the account of Balaam's donkey that spoke in Numbers 22:21-34. Some say that Balaam's donkey spoke by inspiration, or, that God told it what to say. I personally do not think that is accurate. In speaking once with a preacher about the donkey he said, "If God could inspire a donkey and tell him what to say, He could also inspire others." By that he meant the men of Hampton Court. But let's look at the account of Balaam's donkey who spoke.

Again, the recording of this event is found in Numbers 22:21-34. Starting in verses 21 we see Balaam saddling and getting on his donkey to travel with the Princes of Moab. In verses 22-27 we see the angel of the Lord standing in the way of the donkey trying to stop it. The donkey tried to stop but Balaam kept trying to continue on his way not seeing what the donkey could see. In verse 27 it says, "And when the ass saw the angel of the LORD, she fell down under Balaam: and Balaam's anger was kindled, and he smote the ass with a staff." Then in verse 28 it says, "And the LORD opened the mouth of the ass, and she said unto Balaam, What have I done unto thee, that thou hast smitten me these three times?" Notice what this verse says and what it does not say. It says, "the Lord opened the mouth of the ass…" That was all He did, God made it possible for the ass to speak. Then it says, "…and SHE said unto Balaam…" It does not say thus saith the Lord or say thus to Balaam. It says SHE said to Balaam.

I said above that this was the recording of this event! Again, God's part of it was He opened the mouth of the ass. In other words, He made it possible for the ass to speak. John Gill wrote about this, "This was a very extraordinary and miraculous affair, and effected by a supernatural power, that a dumb creature, which had not organs endued with speech, should speak so plainly and distinctly, as is after expressed; and yet it should not be thought incredible, for what is it that Omnipotence cannot do?"

Another writer wrote, "(God) conferred upon her the power of speech and reasoning for that time. The ass spoke!"

The reasoning of the man who said, "If God could inspire a donkey and tell her what to say, He could inspire others." In other words, it was God Who, like David and all the others He used to write the words of God's Word, told the ass what to say. If that is true, and I do not believe it is, then God also told the serpent what to say in Genesis. What did the serpent say? What was the conversation between the serpent and Eve? I will highlight the words of the serpent who we know is Satan. Genesis 3:1-5 says,

> *"Now the serpent was more subtil than any beast of the field which the LORD God had made.* ***And he said unto the woman, Yea, hath God said, Ye shall not eat of every tree of the garden?*** *And the*

CHAPTER 10: WHAT ABOUT DUAL AND TRIPLE INSPIRATION?

woman said unto the serpent, We may eat of the fruit of the trees of the garden: But of the fruit of the tree which is in the midst of the garden, God hath said, Ye shall not eat of it, neither shall ye touch it, lest ye die. **And the serpent said unto the woman, Ye shall not surely die: For God doth know that in the day ye eat thereof, then your eyes shall be opened, and ye shall be as gods, knowing good and evil."**

Would God cause Eve to doubt what He said? (Hath God said?) Would God change what He said originally to tempt Eve to sin? (Ye shall not eat of every tree of the garden?) Would God tell the serpent to lie? (Ye shall not surely die.) Would God say what He said tempting Eve to "be as gods?" I do not believe it was God Who told the serpent what to say because He would then be going against His own Word. James 1:13 " Let no man say when he is tempted, I am tempted of God*: **for God cannot be tempted with evil, neither tempteth he any man**:*"

I do not believe it was God Who told the serpent what to say but it was God, Who by inspiration, told the writer (Moses) what was said and they recorded it. The same is true in the conversations we see multitudes of times in the Bible between individuals. What they said in those conversations was not what God told everyone to say in many cases, they were conversations between people that God recorded by inspiration for us to see and learn from. If He told the serpent and the ass what to say, and if all conversations in the Bible are what God told everyone to say then he would have told some people to lie when He is against telling lies, He would have told people to blaspheme when He is against blasphemy. No, this is not what happened. What God did was to record the conversation the donkey and the serpent had by inspiration. God TOLD the writers what was said and they wrote it down.

In an internet conversation with a proponent of the dual inspiration teaching he said, "...the Holy Spirit guided the translators to choose the right words, the King James Bible is also inspired." I then said, "Then you believe in dual inspiration." Then he denied he believes in dual inspiration but what he said tells me otherwise.

Let's see what some others have written about dual inspiration.

Mickey Carter in his book <u>Things That Are Different Are Not the Same</u> on page 149 wrote,

> "You cannot find translating committees with the personal spirituality and dedication of that of the King James Bible translating committee. God was in the selection of the translators. He did not inspire them (dual inspiration) as He did Paul, but He did superintend and guard over them to preserve His word."

He also wrote,

> "It is easy to look back and see that God's hand was in the work, not in the sense of inspiration (dual inspiration) but in having that which had already been inspired translated and correctly preserved. (Page 161)

In an article from the <u>Baptist Magazine</u> the July/August edition on page 23, Dr. Shelton Smith the Editor of the Sword of the Lord paper we asked,

> "Do you believe in dual inspiration?"

He replied,

> "No, I do not! The Bible was inspired at the time of its writing. That is the claim of Scripture itself...God has preserved His Word for us."

Dr. Jack Hyles wrote,

CHAPTER 10: WHAT ABOUT DUAL AND TRIPLE INSPIRATION?

"We know that the inspired words of God have been preserved. They were original in inspiration and Divine in preservation. **God inspired His words one time!** …the King James Bible is the preserved Word of God! The Bible I hold in my hand and the words are preserved!"

Dr. David Brown of the King James Bible Research Council wrote in an article,

"We believe that God inspired His words once and that God has preserved His words in the Hebrew, Aramaic Masoretic Text of the Old Testament and the Traditional Text of the New Testament. This brings me to these questions, Did God again speak (dual inspiration) to the King James translators in like fashion as He spoke through Moses, David, Isaiah, Paul or John? Or, did God re-inspire the King James translators?" (Now he quotes Dr. David Sorenson) "The answer to that question should be apparent. **There is absolutely no record of claim that the King James translators, erudite and godly as they they were, received any such second inspiration. A careful study of their work and the subsequent publishing process absolutely militates against such notion.**"

Then Dr. Brown reiterates,

*"As stated earlier, God inspired His words only when they flowed from the tip of the pens of the various Scriptural authors. He has not done so again, **We do not believe in double inspiration of any type, no matter who promotes it.**"*

Dr. Brown also wrote,

> "The King James Bible translators had God's preserved words in front of them as they worked with the Hebrew Masoretic text and the Greek Traditional text. They did not need to be re-inspired, they simple needed to faithfully and accurately translated those preserved words and that is what they did! That outcome is the Kings James Bible is God's Word kept intact in English."

Dr. Phil Stringer who is the Vice President of the King James Bible Research Council writes,

> "I do not believe that the King James Bible is inspired. (dual inspiration) Inspiration happened only once; that is when God took control of a person and spoke His words through them or caused them to write down His words. That is not because I believe that there is any weakness or any inferiority in the King James Bible. I believe the King James Bible is perfect and inerrant! There is nothing about the King James Bible that needs to be corrected or improved. But, God inspired His words only once…He has not done it again!"

In my message I gave to the National King James Bible Research Council meeting and in a letter I wrote to an ex-Pastor I said,

> "If by the phrase the King James Bible is inspired you mean that the men who translated the Word of God to the English were inspired (dual inspiration), I do not believe that. The inspiration took place to the Holy men of old who were moved by the Holy Spirit and that inspiration ended with the last word of the last sentence of the Book of Revelation. They have been preserved since then. The translators never claimed

CHAPTER 10: WHAT ABOUT DUAL AND TRIPLE INSPIRATION?

inspiration (which will be proven in the translation section of this book from their own writing), and nowhere in the Scriptures does God attribute that to them. If by the phrase the King James Bible is inspired you mean that the infallible, inerrant and preserved Word of God is there in its entirety by faithful, and accurate translation, then that is what I believe. The King James Bible it the preserved Word of God!"

In another article by Dr. Stringer for the KJBRC entitled, <u>The King James Only Baptist Civil War over Inspiration</u> he wrote,

> "Faithful translations of the words given by inspiration have all the authority and Holy Spirit power of the originals. Faithful translations of Scripture are Scripture. However, the Bible calls this preservation not derivative inspiration."

The men of Hampton Court never one time referred to themselves as being inspired, they understood the difference in translation and inspiration and many times in their letter to the readers they stated their job was to **translate**. More will be said about this in the section on translation. They understood the process and as I have said many times in preaching and teaching about the process, "The difference between Moses and the men of Hampton Court is a blank piece of paper!" What I mean is this, when Moses heard the voice of God as God spoke to him the words of the Pentateuch, Moses did not know what God would say until God spoke. He would then write and speak what God told him to write and speak. The same is true with all the other writers God used to give the Scriptures to. They all started out with a blank piece of paper so to speak. But, when the men of Hampton Court set before them the Hebrew and Greek manuscripts, and the other translations to do their work, all that God has said was already written down by the writers and then passed down through the work of the scribes and others before them, So, the original writers of Scripture wrote as God-breathed the words of the Word of God. They started out with a blank page. The translators had all that had been already written and therefore did not need to be re-inspired. It was all already before them, it just had to be translated!

In my message to the National King James Bible Research Council I asked some important questions at the end of the message. But first, I read to them the 15 rules Richard Bancroft laid out for them at the beginning of their work of translation called, "Richard Bancroft's Rules to be Observed in the Translation of the Bible." They are as follows…(and you will see them again)

1. The ordinary Bible read in the church, commonly called the Bishops' Bible, to be followed, and as little altered as the truth of the original will permit.

2. The names of the prophets, and the holy writers, with the other names in the text, to be retained as near as may be, accordingly as they are vulgarly used.

3. The old ecclesiastical words to be kept, namely, as the word church not to be translated congregation &c.

4. When any word hath divers significations, that to be kept which hath been most commonly used by the most eminent Fathers, being agreeable to the propriety of the place, and the analogy of faith.

5. The division of the chapters to be altered either not at all, or as little as may be, if necessity so require.

CHAPTER 10: WHAT ABOUT DUAL AND TRIPLE INSPIRATION?

6. No marginal notes at all to be affixed, but only for the explanation of the Hebrew or Greek words, which cannot without some circumlocution so briefly and fitly be expressed in the text.

7. Such quotations of places to be marginally set down, as shall serve for the fit reference of one Scripture to another.

8. Every particular man of each company to take the same chapter or chapters; and having translated or amended them severally by himself, where he thinks good, all to meet together, confer what they have done, and agree for their part what shall stand.

9. As any one company hath dispatched any one book in this manner, they shall send it to the rest, to be considered of seriously and judiciously; for his Majesty is very careful in this point.

10. If any company, upon the review of the book so sent, shall doubt or differ upon any places, to send them word thereof, note the places, and therewithal send their reasons; to which if they consent not, the difference to be compounded at the general meeting, which is to be of the chief persons of each company, at the end of the work.

11. When any place of special obscurity is doubted of, letters to be directed by authority, to send to any learned man in the land for his judgment in such a place.

12. Letters to be sent from every Bishop to the rest of his clergy, admonishing them of this Translation in hand; and to move and

charge as many as, being skilful in the tongues, have taken pains in that kind, to send his particular observations to the company, either at Westminster, Cambridge, or Oxford.

13. The directors in each company to be the Deans of Westminster and Chester, for that place; and the King's Professors in the Hebrew and Greek in either University.

14. These translations to be used, when they agree better with the text than the Bishops' Bible: Tyndale's, Matthew's, Coverdale's, Whitchurch's [Great], Geneva.

15. Besides the said directions before mentioned, three or four of the most ancient and grave divines in either of the Universities, not employed in translating, to be assigned by the Vice-Chancellor, upon conference with the rest of the Heads, to be overseers of the Translations, as well Hebrew as Greek, for the better observation of the fourth rule above specified.

My questions and statements were as follow, If the men of Hampton Court were inspired…

- Why did it take them 7 years (1604-1611) to complete the work?
- Why 6 different companies to translate and compare their work among themselves? (#8-10)
- Why compare their work to previous translations? (#1, 14)
- Why did they consult with other people outside their company? (#11, 12)
- Why didn't they say they were inspired like the Prophets and Apostles? "…WE SET BEFORE US TO TRANSLATE BEING THE TONGUES WHEREIN GOD WAS PLEASED TO SPEAK TO HIS CHURCH BY HIS PROPHETS AND APOSTLES."

CHAPTER 10: WHAT ABOUT DUAL AND TRIPLE INSPIRATION?

- Why did they say they revised their work? (Opening statement – "Translated out of the original tongues and with the former translations diligently compared and revised by His Majesty's special command."
- They indicated it took much time to do the work of translation.
- They understood the process.
- They knew what translation work was.
- They said they translated out of the original tongues.

My main question is, if they were inspired, or if dual inspiration was the process, why all the rules? Why? Did Moses have similar rules? Did others check and re-check the work of Matthew? Were there different teams to cross check the things John wrote? Inspiration, preservation and translation are all different and are all a part of the process which the men of Hampton Court understood. More could be asked and said but I will close this chapter and section with this, The Word of God was given by inspiration of God…God-breathed the words as He spoke them to the men He used to write them. Now we have the verbal and plenary inspired Word of God by meticulous preservation and faithful and accurate translation in the King James Bible keeping all the infallibility, inerrancy and authority of what God originally inspired or spoke. Inspiration is not what God did to the Scriptures, it is how He GAVE THEM!

Section 4
Preservation

"By extension, it was WORDS that God gave by inspiration, and it is those WORDS God gave that are preserved." Psalm 12:7

Dr. Gary L. Mann

Chapter 11

Preservation

1 Peter 1:25

> *"But the word of the Lord endureth for ever. And this is the word which by the gospel is preached unto you."*

John Gill wrote about this verse,

> "Though men die, and ministers of the word too, and everything in the world is uncertain, unstable, fleeting, and passing away, and whatever change has been in the ordinances of divine service; yet the word of the Lord, the Gospel of Christ, is settled for ever, and will never pass away:"

Those who teach that inspiration is the breath of God in the Scriptures, not only ignore the Holy Spirit, but they also ignore the promises of God in the Bible to preserve His words. They teach continuous inspiration meaning that the breath of God continues in the Scriptures and that without that breath, "We will never have any scripture except in some old, dead languages." They again have the wrong understanding of what Biblical inspiration is, God's Word is God breathed, He spoke every word to the writers of Scripture. All Scripture is GIVEN (how?) BY INSPIRATION OF GOD. Inspiration is not what God did to the Scriptures but how He gave the Scriptures. In their teaching, they accuse us, based on their wrong understanding of inspiration, of teaching heresy. They say that if only the originals were inspired (their definition), then since we do not have the originals then we do not have God's Word. This denies preservation! But, since they started out with a wrong definition of inspiration they then move on to the incorrect understanding of preservation. (Continuous and Preserved inspiration) Their teaching of preserved inspiration is not that the words of the Word of God are preserved, but that the breath of God is what is preserved, thus "preserved" inspiration.

In a set of emails I have in my possession from a known preacher who is a leader in the wrong teaching about inspiration and preservation, are his comments about preservation and how it changed from 2008 to 2010 during the time he resigned as the Pastor. I will mention them again later in detail but for now I want to start out with a definition and the historical process of preservation.

The word preservation means, "the act of preserving or keeping safe from destruction or decay. To keep in its original state." You are familiar with canning tomatoes or other items. There is a process to go through so the lid of the jar will seal to keep the contents safe from destruction or decay. The process keeps the contents in its original state. We call them preserved or preserves. God wants His Word to be pure for all peoples of all times. What He said to Moses is still in print today and has been kept safe from destruction and decay. It has been kept in its original state both in the Hebrew and English. We continue to have God's Word by preservation!

We know and understand that God breathed the words of the Word of God to Moses through John and that those parchments they originally wrote on no longer exist. By the way, don't let the critics keep you from talking about the originals and the original languages, the men of Hampton Court mentioned them often.

Jeremiah was commanded by God in **Jeremiah30:1&2**,

"The word that came to Jeremiah from the LORD, saying, Thus speaketh the LORD God of Israel, saying, **Write thee all the words that I have spoken unto thee in a book."**

THAT IS INSPIRATION! Now in order for us to have those words, they somehow had to get from the time Jeremiah

CHAPTER 11: PRESERVATION

wrote them to now. THAT IS PRESERVATION. Notice again Jeremiah was told by God to write down all the WORDS I HAVE SPOKEN TO YOU IN A BOOK. The words were God-breathed, they were spoken by God! Verses three and four state the reason God wanted these words in a book,

> *"For, lo, the days come, saith the LORD, that I will bring again the captivity of my people Israel and Judah, saith the LORD: and I will cause them to return to the land that I gave to their fathers, and they shall possess it. And these are the words that the LORD spake concerning Israel and concerning Judah."*

The people of Israel and Judah would return someday and God wanted it written so they in the future could see what God told Jeremiah. In order for this to happen those words had to be protected, they had to be preserved! There are some other verses you should see here also.

Jeremiah 36:2

> *"Take thee a roll of a book, and write therein all the words that I have spoken unto thee against Israel, and against Judah, and against all the nations, from the day I spake unto thee, from the days of Josiah, even unto this day."*

Isaiah 51:16

> *"And I have put my words in thy mouth, and I have covered thee in the shadow of mine hand, that I may plant the heavens, and lay the foundations of the earth, and say unto Zion, Thou art my people."*

Isaiah 59:21

> *"As for me, this is my covenant with them, saith the LORD; My spirit that is upon thee, and my words which I have put in thy mouth, shall not*

depart out of thy mouth, nor out of the mouth of thy seed, nor out of the mouth of thy seed's seed, saith the LORD, from henceforth and for ever."

That last verse is an interesting one when you read what John Gill had to say about it. He wrote as follows. "**As for me, this is my covenant with them, saith the Lord,**.... Which shall be manifested and made good to them that repent of their sins, and, believe in Christ; and to whom the particular blessing of it shall be applied, the forgiveness of their sins; see Rom 11:27, **my Spirit which is upon thee, and my words which I have put in thy mouth**; the Spirit of God, with his gifts and graces, which were upon Christ the Redeemer without measure; and the doctrines he received from his divine Father to teach others, and which he gave to his apostles; the same Spirit which in measure was put upon them, **and the same truths which were delivered to them:**

shall not depart out of thy mouth, nor out of the mouth of thy seed, nor out of the mouth of thy seed's seed, saith the Lord, from henceforth and for ever; that is, *shall always continue with the church and her spiritual seed, such as are born in her, and brought up by her, throughout all successive ages, and to the end of time;* and it may be observed, that after the conversion of the Jews, to which this prophecy has a special regard, they shall no more apostatize; the Spirit of the Lord shall not depart from them; and the Gospel shall always be professed by them: and it may be further observed, that the Spirit and the word go together; and that the latter is only effectual as accompanied will, the former, and is a proof of the perseverance of the church of God, and of all such who have the Spirit and grace of God, Christ will always have a church, and that church a seed, in which the Spirit and word will always remain. The grace of the Spirit, in the hearts of God's people, never removes from them; nor his Gospel from such, in whose hearts it works effectually." Preservation of the words and their teaching!

CHAPTER 11: PRESERVATION

The process of preservation of the Hebrew and Greek was a very tedious and exacting process. The Hebrew Scriptures were basically protected and preserved by the Aaronic priesthood and the Greek, along then with the Hebrew manuscripts, were copied and preserved by scribes and others. As parchments got old and well used, they would have to be hand copied before they were too far gone. There would also be parchments copied for people so they could have a copy of the Scriptures also as in the case with Phillip and the Ethiopian eunuch.

You can imagine how time consuming and difficult it would be to copy letter for letter and word for word anything that was already on parchment. To copy the words of the Word of God was a very daunting and challenging task and it would be done to specific rules. I have them below.

- Parchments must be made from the skin of animals only.
- Parchments must be prepared by Jews only.
- Parchment must be bound together by strings taken from clean animals only.
- Each column of writing must have between them between 48 and 60 lines only. Rolls must have the same number of columns consistently throughout, and each column was to be exactly 30 letters wide.
- Each column must be lined first, and if 3 words were written down without a line, the whole copy is made worthless and destroyed.
- The fifth Book of Moses, must terminate exactly with a line.
- Ink must be black only and made to a recipe.
- Scribes must be clothed in full scribal dress.
- No word or letter can be written from memory. The scribe must have an authentic copy before him, and must read and pronounce each word out loud before writing it.

- Pens must be wiped reverently each time the word "God" is written.
- The scribe must wash his whole body before writing the Name of God (Jehovah).
- Strict rules apply dealing with the use of the pen, shapes of the letters, and spaces between letters, words and sections.
- Rolls must be checked and revised within 30 days or the whole roll becomes worthless.
- One mistake condemns the sheet.
- Three mistakes on any page condemns the whole manuscript.
- Every word and letter must be counted, If one letter is missing, is added, or touches another the whole manuscript must be destroyed.
- Between each consonant, a hair's breadth; between each section, the breadth of nine consonants; between each book three lines.

As you can see it was quite a process to copy from one manuscript to another. Thankfully we have computers, printing presses and copiers! But what you see above was the job of the priest or scribe. It was truly an art and a solemn undertaking. This process is how we have over 5,500 manuscripts and many more tens of thousands fragments of manuscripts which underlie the Antioch line of manuscripts. And, this is the process that brought about the 35 or so Alexandrian manuscripts. Please note the difference in how many manuscripts are in the Antioch line and the Alexandrian line of manuscripts, it is important for later.

From his book <u>Things That Are Different Are Not the Same</u>, Dr. Mickey Carter wrote the following on pages 116 and 117,

> "Many times the Hebrew priests translated blindly, but faithfully, they wrote it anyway. That is what is missing with modern translators. They think they pretty well understand the Bible. As

CHAPTER 11: PRESERVATION

they write, they write down what they think it teaches. But the old priesthood copied it accurately, even when he did not understand it."

He went on to write,

"The scribes were so meticulous in their work that they developed a code of rules to follow (as mentioned on the previous page) in order to avoid the possibility of scribal error."

This system or set of rules for copying manuscripts, which will be abbreviated mss. from now on, is vital in your understanding of the differences between the Antioch line of manuscripts which includes the Hebrew Masoretic mss. which is the Hebrew basis for the Old Testament and the Received Text, also known as the Textus Receptus, which is the Greek being the basis for the New Testament in the King James Bible and the corrupted Alexandrian mss which are the basis for all the versions. (ASV, RSV, ESV and others.)

Not only were the priests and scribes responsible to copy the Word of God but the Kings were commanded to also copy the Word of God. Deuteronomy 17:18-20 tells us this and why he was to do so. **"And it shall be, when he sitteth upon the throne of his kingdom, that he shall write him a copy of this law in a book out of *that which is* before the priests the Levites:** And it shall be with him, and he shall read therein all the days of his life: that he may learn to fear the LORD his God, to keep all the words of this law and these statutes, to do them: That his heart be not lifted up above his brethren, and that he turn not aside from the commandment, *to* the right hand, or *to* the left: to the end that he may prolong *his* days in his kingdom, he, and his children, in the midst of Israel." I wonder how many copies there were made by the kings?

In **Acts 8:26 through 39** we see the account of Philip and the Ethiopian eunuch. It reads as follows,

AND WHAT MARVEL!

"And the angel of the Lord spake unto Philip, saying, Arise, and go toward the south unto the way that goeth down from Jerusalem unto Gaza, which is desert. And he arose and went: and, behold, a man of Ethiopia, an eunuch of great authority under Candace queen of the Ethiopians, who had the charge of all her treasure, and had come to Jerusalem for to worship, Was returning, and **sitting in his chariot read Esaias the prophet.** *Then the Spirit said unto Philip, Go near, and join thyself to this chariot. And Philip ran thither to him, and heard him read the prophet Esaias, and said, Understandest thou what thou readest? And he said, How can I, except some man should guide me? And he desired Philip that he would come up and sit with him. The place of the scripture which he read was this, He was led as a sheep to the slaughter; and like a lamb dumb before his shearer, so opened he not his mouth: In his humiliation his judgment was taken away: and who shall declare his generation? for his life is taken from the earth. And the eunuch answered Philip, and said, I pray thee, of whom speaketh the prophet this? of himself, or of some other man? Then Philip opened his mouth, and began at the same scripture, and preached unto him Jesus. And as they went on their way, they came unto a certain water: and the eunuch said, See, here is water; what doth hinder me to be baptized? And Philip said, If thou believest with all thine heart, thou mayest. And he answered and said, I believe that Jesus Christ is the Son of God. And he commanded the chariot to stand still: and they went down both into the water, both Philip and the eunuch; and he baptized him. And when they were come up out of the water, the Spirit of the Lord*

CHAPTER 11: PRESERVATION

caught away Philip, that the eunuch saw him no more: and he went on his way rejoicing."

The Ethiopian eunuch had gone to Jerusalem to worship. While there he purchased a copy of Esaias or the Book of Isaiah. The Book of Isaiah was written somewhere between 760 and 698 B.C. So here we are some **700 years later** and this man is reading Isaiah. Was it the original? Very doubtful. It was a copy of the Book of Isaiah! It had been preserved through the process of copying letter for letter and word for word!

Let me insert this question right here. Were the priests and scribes inspired? Did they write down the words of the Word of God as He told them? It was Scripture and, according to some, since it says that **ALL SCRIPTURE IS GIVEN BY INSPIRATION OF GOD**, which is their mantra to prove the translators were inspired since it says ALL Scripture, in order for them to be consistent with their present day teaching that the men of Hampton Court were inspired, shouldn't the priests and scribes also have been inspired? It says ALL Scripture! Here is another question, if the priests and scribes were inspired, again, why the rules?! By the way, nowhere have I ever heard anyone say, nor have I seen written anywhere that the priests and scribes were inspired. Nowhere! Why? Because they weren't! They faithfully and articulately copied letter for letter and word for word using the system already mentioned. This was a part of the process of preservation. They were meticulous in their work!

Paul stopped in Thessalonica and, as was his usual method he, "...went in unto them, and three sabbath days **reasoned with them out of the scriptures**, Opening and alleging, that Christ must needs have suffered, and risen again from the dead; and that this Jesus, whom I preach unto you, is Christ." (Acts 17:2 & 3) What Scriptures did he reason with them out of? They were in Thessalonica, not Jerusalem. They had copies there also and the people were familiar with the Scriptures! There were many, many copies of Scripture all over the place!

I do not remember where I found this quote but a man named John Owen once said, "But yet we affirm, that the whole Word of God in every letter…as given from Him by inspiration, is preserved without corruption." And I say, AMEN!

Chapter 12
Preservation, An Important Part of the Process

Matthew 24:35

> *"Heaven and earth shall pass away, but my words shall not pass away."*

Acts 8:30a

> *"And Philip ran thither to him, and heard him read the prophet Esaias,"*

2 Timothy 3:15

> *"And that from a child thou hast known the holy scriptures, which are able to make thee wise unto salvation through faith which is in Christ Jesus."*

Here are three verses which indicate a preservation of the words of the Word of God. The first one is Jesus Himself promising that what He was saying then, and by extension all He has said, would never pass away The second one I mentioned previously where the Ethiopian eunuch was reading chapter 53 out of a copy of the Book of Isaiah. The last one is where Paul tells Timothy that THE SCRIPTURES WHICH HE HAD KNOWN SINCE CHILDHOOD were able to make him wise unto salvation. In order to have known those Old Testament Scriptures and possibly the ones he had read of the New Testament, they had to have been in existence. What is a great thought is that Timothy could have read some of the originals from what Paul had been inspired to write.

Basically, the process on how we now have the Word of God is a three-fold process. First there is inspiration, next is preservation and lastly translation. Preservation is a very important part of the process whereby we have the inspired Word of God for all generations. To say, as some have recently taught, that the words of His Word have not been preserved is just not so. Neither is the teaching that it is simply the breath of God in the words that has been preserved. That too is not so as I have written earlier. And then for some to teach that the English somehow CORRECTS the Hebrew and Greek is also not so. If the English corrected the Hebrew and the Greek then that in itself denies the doctrine of preservation and smacks at the promises of God that His word would be there for all generations. God must have made a big mistake by speaking to people in their languages (Hebrew or Greek) if the English corrects those languages. And, if the English corrects the Greek then there was not an infallible, inerrant Bible until 1611!

The process is that originally God-breathed, or spoke His words to Moses through John, Genesis through Revelation. The materials used by Moses to record those words and all the other holy men of old wrote what God breathed. Those materials could not last on which they penned the words God breathed. Therefore, as mentioned before, and I will quickly re-cap the process in this chapter the process of preservation of the Scriptures became necessary. So, today there are 5000 plus manuscripts and over 30,000 fragments of manuscripts in existence that has all Scripture in the original languages and then there are now also many translations into other langugues. More will be said about that in the translation section.

Inspiration happened when God-breathed the words. In **Jeremiah 30:2** is a perfect example of what happened when God inspired His words. **"Thus speaketh the LORD God of Israel, saying, Write thee all the words that I have spoken unto thee in a book."** Here are some more examples of the process of inspiration and preservation.

CHAPTER 12: AN IMPORTANT PART OF THE PROCESS

Jeremiah 36:2

> *"Take thee a roll of a book, and write therein all the words that I have spoken unto thee against Israel, and against Judah, and against all the nations, from the day I spake unto thee, from the days of Josiah, even unto this day."*

Psalm 33:11

> *"The counsel of the LORD standeth for ever, the thoughts of his heart to all generations."*

Psalm 119:160

> *"Thy word is true from the beginning: and every one of thy righteous judgments endureth for ever."*

Isaiah 30:8

> *"Now go, write it before them in a table, and note it in a book, that it may be for the time to come for ever and ever:"*

Isaiah 40:8

> *"The grass withereth, the flower fadeth: but the word of our God shall stand for ever."*

Dr. Thomas Strous puts inspiration this way,

> "Inspiration is the process whereby the Holy Spirit led the writers of Scripture to record accurately His very words; the product of the process was an inspired (God-breathed) original."

A friend of mine, Dr. H.D. Williams, wrote about inspiration in his book <u>The Miracle of Inspiration</u> this way,

> "Inspiration is the miracle whereby the Words of Scripture in Hebrew, Aramaic and Greek were God-breathed and once delivered using the holy men of God and their vocabulary, who perfectly

recorded them once as they were moved along by the Holy Spirit in such a way that all the Words written are infallible and inerrant in the sixty-six books of the canon of Scripture." I think we understand now what inspiration is!

God gave all Scripture by inspiration and we now have what God-breathed by the process of accurate copies (preservation) and accurate translation making what we read in the King James Bible the preserved Word of God which is still infallible and inerrant having all the authority behind it just like the originals. The Holy Spirit uses the words of the Word of God and is the power behind the words of the Word of God. One very famous preacher from the past put it this way, and I have his voice on an old computer saying this, "Originally inspired, divinely preserved." I will come back to this man later for a very specific reason which I will reveal then.

The process of preservation took place when men, as taught in the previous chapter, laboriously copied letter for letter and word for word from one parchment to another, and then others then carefully translated from those parchments into a receptor language (Latin, Syrian, German, English, Spanish and many others). Again, John Owen said "But we affirm, that the whole Word of God in every letter...as given from Him by inspiration, is PRESERVED WITHOUT CORRPUTION." ***EVERY LETTER!!***

But we will see later in another chapter, the true preservation of all God said hit a snag in a place called Alexandria. But, thankfully there is another place named Antioch in Syria, where God's Word was correctly handled as in many other places through time and we have their work in the 35,000 plus manuscripts and fragments where the Word of God had been accurately copied and preserved. We will look at those two streams of manuscripts later. For now, I want to insert here some quotes about preservation which comes from previous and present day men, men who taught me and others who wrote their

CHAPTER 12: AN IMPORTANT PART OF THE PROCESS

thoughts on this subject and I will continue to teach the SAME things.

From Dr. David Brown, Ph.D in his material <u>What Inspiration is Not</u> are the following quotes.

> "The natural question is, if we do not have the originals, do we have the Word of God? The answer is yes! God HAS PRESERVED HIS WORD!" (Page 12)

> "Has God preserved His Word perfect for us today, or was it only perfect in the 'original' autographs? If God has not preserved His Word perfectly, we must assume that we are preaching and teaching from a book that is not completely reliable as the 'original' autographs are no longer accessible. Our King James Bible, because of its meticulous and accurate translation of the preserved words of God maintains all the authority of the Holy Spirit power..." (Page 15)

He then quotes Dean John Burgon who wrote,

> "There exists no reason for supposing that (God) who in first instance thus gave to mankind the Scriptures of Truth, straightway abdicated His office; took no further care of His work; abandoned those writings to their fate." (Page 12)

On page 13 he then says before he quotes the London Baptist Confession of 1677 and 1689, "I hold to what Baptists have historically held to. God has preserved His words as He promised. The London Baptist Confession says, 'The Old Testament in Hebrew, (which was the native language of the people of God of old), and the New Testament Greek (which at the time of writing of it was most generally known to the nations) being immediately inspired of God, and by His singular care and providence are kept pure in all ages and are therefore authentical..."' I too hold to those same teachings and beliefs of what "Baptists have historically held to."

From the book, <u>Which Greek Text?</u> By Charles L. Surrett and published in Kings Mountain, North Carolina in 1999 by Surrett Family Publishers on page 42 is the following,

> "Why would God go to the trouble of breathing out words (inspiration) that were meticulously written down, if they were to be soon lost?"

Again, in Dr. Mickey's book <u>Things That Are Different Are Not the Same</u> on page 161 he wrote,

> "It is easy to look back and see that God's hand was in the work, Not in the sense of inspiration, but in having that which had already been inspired translated and correctly preserved."

Dr. Shelton Smith in the Baptist Magazine July/August 2008 issue answered the question,

> "Do you believe in dual inspiration?" [His answer was,] "No, I do not! The Bible was inspired at the time of its writing. That is the claim of Scripture itself...God has preserved His Word for us. It is preserved in the Hebrew Masoretic text and in the Greek Textus Receptus. It is also preserved for us in English in the King James Bible. What He first inspired, the Lord God has now preserved. Therefore, when I hold the King James Bible in my hand, I hold the inspired text. It was inspired, and now that inspired Word had been protected, preserved and provided for us."

In a blog by one who I believe does not blog anymore I found, "God used the tool of inspiration to deliver His pure words to man and then preserves those words for each generation. Each generation had been promised by God to have a copy of His pure Word. This does not mean that man (and Satan) will not try to

CHAPTER 12: AN IMPORTANT PART OF THE PROCESS

corrupt God's Word. They have been doing this since th Garden of Eden and will continue to do so. But God did not promise that men would not try to corrupt His words. He promised that He would preserve His pure words to each generation."

As previously promised, I am now going to quote a preacher who is very well known. The reason I am doing this is because a man who teaches the preserved and continuous inspiration teachings and that the men of Hampton Court were just as inspired as Moses and Paul, and who teaches it is, and I quote from his blog site, "…**not just preserved words otherwise there is no life in those words. It is preserved inspiration that makes the Words live and become incorruptible seed that when placed into the soul of a man, woman, boy or girl causes the new birth.**" and he is a staunch defender and promoter of this famous preacher who passed away not too many years ago that does not teach preserved inspiration. The famous preacher is one everyone knows and has an opinion about. The famous preacher that I will now extensively quote is Dr. Jack Hyles, who, by the way, was also my pastor for four years while I attended college. The first set of quotes come from Dr. Hyles writing titled, <u>The Need for an Every Word Bible.</u>

"God has **preserved His words** for us in the King James Bible." (Page 51)

"If God could **preserve His words** for 4000 years when they had no printing presses at all, don't you think He could **preserve the words** of God for 2000 years with our modern way of printing?" (Page 58)

"That revelation which God inspired **has been preserved** as He said He would preserve it for these 6000 years which means **we still have those very words**…" (Page 63)

> "**If God did not preserve the Words** of the Bible, then He is a respecter of persons." (Page 67)

> "Is God so weak that he could not **preserve His Words**? Could not God Who gave His Words (inspiration) to holy men of old **preserve His words** for our generation?" (Page 69)

> "Every single word of God has been preserved in the King James Bible…" (Page 97)

> "If I did not believe that every WORD in the Bible had been PRESERVED from the time it was given…I would walk out of this pulpit and I wouldn't waste my life preaching."

> "**God has preserved His words** for us in the King James Bible."

From the last message he preached on the Bible before He died are the following which I have on my old computer and have listened to multiple times.

> "We know that the words of God are available. The originals were not there in David's day yet he knew about what they taught, **yet they had been preserved.**"

> "We know they were originally inspired to the holy men of God."

> "**We know that the inspired words have been preserved.** They were original in inspiration and Divine in preservation. God inspired the words one time. The God Who originally inspired or gave man His words can also work in the lives of men **in preservation of the words of God originally given.**"

CHAPTER 12: AN IMPORTANT PART OF THE PROCESS

"Those words have always been preserved."

"The King James Bible is the preserved Word of God! The Bible I hold in my hand is the King James Bible **and the words are preserved**. I have the very Word of God."

Over and over again in this last message he preached on the Bible before his homegoing he said the King James Bible is the preserved Word of God!

His last statement was,

"Thank God we have the preserved words of God in the King James Bible."

Now, again compare those words with what the other preacher said in his blog…"**It is not just preserved words** otherwise there is no life in those words. It is preserved inspiration that makes the Words live and become incorruptible seed that when placed into the soul of a man, woman, boy or girl causes the new birth." (I will get back to this later and show you the change that took place in his teaching from 2008 to 2010 which again I have the proof directly from his blog site.) To quote a book title here, things that are different are not the same! (Where is a smiley face emoji when you need one?)

Dr. Edward F. Hills stated that the Scriptures have been preserved by God in His providence so that the church would always have the Words as a lamp to her feet and a light to her path."

Dr. Phil Stringer in his article <u>The King James Bible Only Baptist Civil War over Inspiration</u> wrote on page one,

"Let me be crustal clear! I believe that the King James Bible is God's Word KEPT INTACT IN ENGLISH."

Dr. Stringer then quotes John Selden who wrote,

> "The translators in King James time took an excellent way. That part of the Bible was given to him who was most excellent in such a tongue…and then they met together and one read that translation the rest holding in the hands some Bible either of the learned tongues or French, Italian, Spanish, etc. If they found any fault they spoke, if not they read on. Then Dr. Stringer wrote, "This was not the method of King Saul, Malachi, Isaiah, Matthew…when they were inspired of the Lord. It is an example of men being used of God to PRESERVE and transmit His Word."

In all these quotes, except for the one, it is the WORDS that have been preserved. The men I have quoted are far and again more of a scholar and serious student of the Bible and the process before us than the man who only repeated a woman's teaching when he spouts,

> "If the only Scripture that is inspired is that which God 'breathed' (he is being sarcastic), out with His mouth, then we will never have any Scripture except in some old dead language."

(I feel like washing the keyboard every time I type that.) That denies preservation because of his (or should I say her) false teaching on inspiration that it is not the words that are preserved but the breath of God in the words.

The process thus far is very simple. First, God GAVE all Scripture by speaking them (that is called inspiration), to the holy men of old (Moses through John), who then wrote down the words. David said, in 2 Samuel 23:2 "The Spirit of the LORD spake by me, and his word *was* in my tongue." Of this John Gill wrote,

> **"The Spirit of the Lord spake by me**,…. The psalms and songs he composed were not the fruits

CHAPTER 12: AN IMPORTANT PART OF THE PROCESS

of his own genius, **but were written by him under the inspiration of the Spirit of God; by whom holy men of God, the penmen of the Scriptures, spoke, even as they were moved by the Holy Ghost, of whom David was one,** being a prophet; see Act_1:16 Act_2:30; so the Targum here,"David spoke by the spirit of prophecy of the Lord:"or spake "in me" (h); what he spoke was first internally impressed upon his mind by the Spirit of God, and then he expressed it with his tongue, as follows: and his word *was* in my tongue; not only the matter of his psalms was indited by the Spirit of God, and suggested to his mind; **but the very words in which they are delivered were given to him, and he was directed to make use of them, and did."**

Even Baalam understood this process. We find in Numbers **Numbers 22:38** when he appeared before Balak he said,

"And Balaam said unto Balak, Lo, I am come unto thee: have I now any power at all to say any thing? **the word that God putteth in my mouth, that shall I speak."**

Then he said in Numbers 23 verses 4 & 5

"And God met Balaam: and he said unto him, I have prepared seven altars, and I have offered upon every altar a bullock and a ram. **And the LORD put a word in Balaam's mouth, and said, Return unto Balak, and thus thou shalt speak."**

Then in Numbers 23:12 he said,

"And he answered and said, Must I not take heed to speak that which the LORD hath put in my mouth?"

That is all inspiration and is also recorded by inspiration as God told Moses about this and exactly what to write.

This part of the process is also explained by the men of Hampton Court...

> "And what marvel? The original thereof being from heaven, not from earth; the author being God, not man; the inditer, the holy spirit, not the wit of the Apostles or Prophets; the Penmen such as were sanctified from the womb, and endued with a principal portion of God's spirit; the matter, verity, piety, purity, uprightness; the form, God's word, God's testimony, God's oracles, the word of truth, the word of salvation, etc.; the effects, light of understanding, stableness of persuasion, repentance from dead works, newness of life, holiness, peace, joy in the holy Ghost; lastly, the end and reward of the study thereof, fellowship with the Saints, participation of the heavenly nature, fruition of an inheritance immortal, undefiled, and that never shall fade away: Happy is the man that delighteth in the Scripture, and thrice happy that meditateth in it day and night."

Even their explanation flows like a clear, cold mountain stream as it falls down to the valley past rocks and plants. Compared to today's writers, myself included, who struggle with dangling participles and split infinitives. The process is very clear and, as I said earlier very simple. When God spoke, men wrote the words He spoke.

The second part of the process is the process of preservation and that preservation has to do with the preservation of the words God originally spoke. It is the responsibility of the church, the pillar and ground of the truth to preserve His Word. Again, His **Word**! We do that by making sure His Word does not change. This is one reason why it is important that the Antioch

CHAPTER 12: AN IMPORTANT PART OF THE PROCESS

stream of mss. are used and not the Alexandrian. The Antioch line is where the Received Text, also called the Textus Receptus, is from and the King James Bible is a direct result of translation from it. The American Standard Version, the Revised Standard Version and the others come from the Alexandrian line of mss and have, like the Sinaiticus and Vaticanus (Alexandrian type mss.), been changed meaning the versions are also changed. More will be said later.

When Jesus was being tempted by the devil in the wilderness He said in Matthew 4:4, "But he answered and said, It is written, Man shall not live by bread alone, **but by every word that proceedeth out of the mouth of God.**" (Inspiration) As taught by others, if we are to live by every word that proceeded out of the mouth of God, then we must have every word that proceeded out of His mouth. This verse alone spells out inspiration and preservation. But, as I laid out to you in the chapter on salvation, the Bible is a dead book to those who are dead in their trespasses and sins. (Ephesians 2:1) Again, in 1 Corinthians 2:14 it says, "But the natural man receiveth not the things of the Spirit of God: for they are foolishness unto him: neither can he know *them,* because they are spiritually discerned." The Bible also says that Satan has, "...blinded the minds of them which believe not, lest the light of the glorious gospel of Christ, who is the image of God, should shine unto them." (2 Corinthians 4:4b)

But, the Bible becomes a living Book when a person places their faith in Christ alone and is then sealed with the Holy Spirit of promise and are indwelt by Him. (2 Corinthians 1:22; Ephesians 1:13; 4:30; Romans 8:11; 1 Corinthians 3:16) Now, because the Spirit of God dwells in US, NOT THE SCRIPTURES, we then are taught by Him all things from the Word of God which He was used to move on the holy men of old who wrote the words of the Word of God. "But the Comforter, *which is* the Holy Ghost, whom the Father will send in my name, he shall teach you all things, and bring all things to your remembrance, whatsoever I have said unto you." (John 14:26) The Bible comes alive to us, not because the Holy Spirit indwells the Scriptures or that His breath is in the Bible and it actually breathes, but because the Holy Spirit, again, Who gave the words now dwells in us and as we read the Bible He then teaches us from it. Simple as that!

Again, I know I am beating a dead horse here but, those who teach that it is the breath or life of the Scriptures that is preserved also state, "IT IS NOT JUST PRESERVED WORDS, otherwise there is no life in those words." (Written on 4/17/2010) Again, this same man mentioned above used to teach, "God must preserve His inspired WORDS and make THEM available to us...So God has preserved the inspired WORDS of God." (Written in 2008) He then even quoted Psalm 12:6 & 7. He also taught, "...the Textus Receptus in the only text that can qualify as containing the inspired and preserved WORDS of God. The Holy Spirit has the same power to preserve His WORD as He does to inspire His Word." (Again written in 2008) My, my, what a difference a day makes. He claims to have "GROWN" but me thinks I hear GROANING instead. (Where is that emoji??)

    Preservation is again, very simple. The WORDS that God gave by inspiration are preserved and kept intact by the accurate and meticulous copying of the Priests, Kings and scribes as laid out before. In large part, what determines whether or not it was an accurate copy was based on the fear of God and a man doing his job well. The men who copied those parchments were for the most part meticulous in their work understanding the importance of making accurate copies and of what they were copying, the Word of God. Their livelihood depended on their work. If they were sloppy in their work they would get that reputation and lose work. But if they were meticulous in it, they had job security and their work was accurate.

    We have over 5,000 copies of mss and 30,000 fragments of mss. available. We also have the King James Bible translation which I have said recently is an important part of the process of

CHAPTER 12: AN IMPORTANT PART OF THE PROCESS

preservation. Just as the scribes and those who copied the parchments were godly men who showed great respect in their work, the translators were also godly men who also showed great care and diligence in their work of translation.

Our ending up with the King James Bible is a direct result of the inspiration of God being preserved for us in the English language by godly men who worked for up to 7 years with a process that I will show you in the translation section. The process is inspiration and then preservation.

I will end with these two verses from Psalm 12:6 and 7,

*"The **words** of the LORD are pure words: as silver tried in a furnace of earth, purified seven times. Thou shalt keep **them**, O LORD, thou shalt preserve **them** from this generation for ever."*

Let God be true and every man a liar!

Chapter 13

Preservation, the Crux of the Matter

A definition for the word "crux" is, "The decisive or most important point at issue." What is the crux of the matter on preservation? I think it has to be whether or not it has been preserved is the crux of the matter on preservation. We know the words of God's Word were inspired, now, have those words been preserved? Do we have the words of the Word of God? Are they available, or, as some have taught, since we do not have the "originals" then we cannot be sure we actually have the words of the Word of God. (This comes from the Alexandrian, or unbelieving, group.)

While it is true we do not have the originals, and please do not be afraid to use that term especially since the men of Hampton Court used it often in their letter to the readers, if God promised to preserve those words so we could live by every word that proceeds out of the mouth of God, then the crux of the matter is that those words HAVE been preserved. Either that has happened or God "mis-spoke" when He made that promise.

I believe so much that the words of the Word of God have been perfectly preserved I have even said, "While it is true that we no longer have the originals, we do have accurate copies of the originals (by preservation). If it were not for preservation, we would not have the Word of God. So, it is NOT that we do not have the originals that is the problem. Whether or not we have God's inspired words is really based on whether or not they have been preserved." We believe the words of God HAVE been preserved and that the King James Bible is a product of those preserved words. They have been protected and kept in their original state by preservation. We have all the words of the Word of God!

CHAPTER 13: THE CRUX OF THE MATTER

A preacher friend of mine once illustrated the process that had been used to get the Bible to all generations. He had three glasses and a pitcher of water set on the table. From the pitcher he poured a full glass of water into the first glass and said, "The pitcher is God, the water is the Word of God and the first glass is inspiration." The preacher then picked up the full glass and poured the water into the second glass and said, "This second glass is the glass of preservation. It now has the same water from the first glass." He said this meaning that what was originally given by inspiration is now the same that was said by preservation. He then poured the water from the second glass into the third glass and said, "This is the glass of translation which still has the water that was originally poured into the first and second glasses." Inspiration, preservation and translation is a process whereby what God originally spoke has been preserved and translated to have all the words of the Word of God that God originally spoke. Preservation is a part of that process. So, preservation seems to be the crux of the matter for us today. The Word of God has either been preserved through the centuries since originally given, or it comes through everyone being "re-inspired."

The detractors of preservation have used their teaching to twist not only the true meaning of inspiration, but they also deny Biblical preservation! Again, from a teaching on this from his own mouth one man stated,

> "If the only Scripture that is inspired is that which God 'breathed' out (which is not their definition of inspiration), then we will never have any Scripture except in some old dead language."

The meaning is that it is not preserved words in the King James Bible, it is inspired words (dual inspiration) in the King James Bible. Their teaching is that the translators (which they could not be called that if they were inspired like Moses through John) were inspired, it was not the process of preservation. Their preservation, as I have said before, is not the preservation of the words as God said it would be, but the preservation of the breath of God in the Scriptures. One man even said that if the life of the Scriptures is not preserved (the breath in the words) then we do not have a living Bible! I quote from a Bible study that was given on Wednesday May 7, 2008. He also wrote and taught that evening,

> "God's Word is preserved, inspired Words; **not just preserved Words**." (So the inspiration or breath is what is preserved, not the words.)

> "If God's Word is not preserved, inspired Words, it is just a dead Word."

> "God's Word can be accurate in its preservation, but without inspiration (the breath) it is an embalmed Bible."

> "If God's Word is preserved only, then when did it expire? (or quit breathing)"

> "If the Word of God has expired, then Jesus expired on the same date."

The correct definition of inspiration is crucial and the preservation of the words of the Word of God is also crucial. When you have the wrong definition for one the other will also be wrong as in this case. To actually say that the Bible is embalmed if only the words are preserved is also to totally misunderstand the Spirit's part as I discussed previously and is heresy!

The word "preservation" in Webster's 1828 dictionary means,

> "**PRESERVA'TION**, n. The act of preserving or keeping safe; the act of keeping from injury, destruction or decay;"

When we speak of preservation of Scripture, we are talking about that process whereby what God originally said is

CHAPTER 13: THE CRUX OF THE MATTER

kept intact through time. Let's first of all look at some Scripture dealing with preservation of Scripture.

Psalm 33:11

> *"The counsel of the LORD standeth for ever, the thoughts of his heart to all generations."*

Psalm 100:5

> *"For the LORD is good; his mercy is everlasting;* **and his truth endureth to all generations."**

Psalm 119:160

> *"Thy word is true from the beginning: and every one of thy righteous judgments endureth for ever."*

Isaiah 30:8

> *"Now go, write it before them in a table, and note it in a book, that it may be* **for the time to come for ever and ever**:*"*

Isaiah 40:8

> *"The grass withereth, the flower fadeth: but* **the word of our God shall stand for ever."**

Matthew 24:35

> *"Heaven and earth shall pass away, but my words shall not pass away."*

John 10:35

> *"If he called them gods, unto whom the word of God came, and* **the scripture cannot be broken;"**

1 Peter 1:25

> **"But the word of the Lord endureth for ever.** *And this is the word which by the gospel is preached unto you."*

Since the Word of God is promised to endure forever, for all generations; cannot pass away, cannot be broken and shall stand forever, then that means that the preservation of the words of the Words of God had to take place. My question is this, if the Word of God will be there for every generation as promised, then why do some teach we really didn't have the Word of God until 1611 when the English supposedly corrects the Hebrew and Greek? Just a thought!

Some of what is being taught either totally ignores preservation or ridicules it based on their wrong understanding of inspiration. The process of the preservation of the Word of God is very simple as I stated before. God PROMISED His Word would be available to all generations, and He has and will continue to keep that promise. How has the Word of God been preserved? There is no doubt that we do not have the originals that God spoke to Moses through John, but there is a multitude of accurate copies (Antioch stream) of what God spoke. We know that the Priests, scribes and Kings were to copy His Word! And they did it meticulously!

Inspiration is what God did as He spoke His word to the human writers. All Scripture is GIVEN by inspiration of God. The process then of preservation is where the Word of God was kept intact from generation to generation as it was copied and re-copied. The Scripture Timothy learned from and that the Ethiopian eunuch had were copies of copies, not re-inspired copies. The preservation of the words of the Word of God is the crux of the matter!

Not only did the men of Hampton Court (the translators of the King James Bible) look at other translations, but they used the Hebrew and Greek manuscripts that were copies of copies of copies. They set before them the Hebrew and Greek mss. to use in their work of translation of the Word of God to end up with the King James Bible in 1611. The Bible we have today is still the inspired words of God by faithful preservation and translation.

CHAPTER 13: THE CRUX OF THE MATTER

If we have no preservation of the Word of God then we have no accurate translation and we then are without God's Word. The critical text (Alexandrian mss.) are incomplete and therefore the men who use that set of mss. will say that they are still trying to find out all God has said. It is somewhere, but they do not have all of it yet. The mss. the Alexandrian crowd uses do not even agree with each other in the few pages they have. This mean then that the preservation of the words of the Word of God did not and still has not happened as God said it would. Either it is preserved or it is not. Either God promised or He did not. Either we have it or we do not. But I believe God! The preservation of the Word of God is the crux of the matter!

Chapter 14
Antioch and Alexandria

There have always been two lines of thought when it comes to the Bible and the things of God. There is truth and error; faith and doubt; belief and unbelief; there are Christians and the lost; righteousness and sin; God and Satan; Heaven and hell; salvation by faith and salvation by works; orthodox Christianity and false Christianity. The same is true when it has to do with the copies of the inspired words of God. There are two lines of manuscripts; the Antioch stream of manuscripts and the Alexandrian line of manuscripts. We will look at the Antioch line first.

The city of Antioch is located in Syria. Antioch is also mentioned in the following verses.

Acts 11:19-27

> *"Now they which were scattered abroad upon the persecution that arose about Stephen travelled as far as Phenice, and Cyprus, and **Antioch**, preaching the word to none but unto the Jews only. And some of them were men of Cyprus and Cyrene, which, when they were come to **Antioch**, spake unto the Grecians, preaching the Lord Jesus. And the hand of the Lord was with them: and a great number believed, and turned unto the Lord. Then tidings of these things came unto the ears of the church which was in Jerusalem: and they sent forth Barnabas, that he should go as far as **Antioch**. Who, when he came, and had seen the grace of God, was glad, and exhorted them all, that with purpose of heart they would cleave unto the Lord. For he was a good man, and full of the Holy Ghost and of faith: and much people was*

CHAPTER 14: ANTIOCH AND ALEXANDRIA

> *added unto the Lord. Then departed Barnabas to Tarsus, for to seek Saul: And when he had found him, he brought him unto **Antioch**. And it came to pass, that a whole year they assembled themselves with the church, and taught much people. And the disciples were called Christians first in Antioch. And in these days came prophets from Jerusalem unto **Antioch**."*

Acts 13:1

> *"Now there were in the church that was at **Antioch** certain prophets and teachers; as Barnabas, and Simeon that was called Niger, and Lucius of Cyrene, and Manaen, which had been brought up with Herod the tetrarch, and Saul."*

Acts 15:22

> *"Then pleased it the apostles and elders, with the whole church, to send chosen men of their own company to **Antioch** with Paul and Barnabas; namely, Judas surnamed Barsabas, and Silas, chief men among the brethren:"*

Acts 15:35

> *"Paul also and Barnabas continued in **Antioch**, teaching and preaching the word of the Lord, with many others also."*

Antioch was a very busy place which was heavily involved in the Gospel. Look at the name of some of the people who were either located there or who went there. There was Barnabas, Saul who we know as Paul, Simeon, Lucius, Manaen, Judas, and Silas. Some of these names are familiar and a few are not. It was also a place where those who had been scattered from Jerusalem ended up in preaching the Gospel and some prophets and others went to Antioch. Very interesting to note that Paul, who God used to write two thirds of the New Testament, spent a lot of time there and considered Antioch his home and the church there his "local church." One person wrote of Antioch, "Here was the springboard for the Gentile church. Just as Jerusalem was the center for the Jewish Christians, Antioch became the hub for the Gentile Christians and the ministry of Paul." It is very, very crucial to remember that Paul spent a lot of time in Antioch which is mentioned at one point where it says, "And it came to pass, that a whole year they assembled themselves with the church, and taught much people." And, again, Paul was used to write most of the New Testament.

We know that Paul believed,

- In the inspiration of the Scriptures – **2 Timothy 3:16**

"All scripture is given by inspiration of God, and is profitable for doctrine, for reproof, for correction, for instruction in righteousness:"

- In salvation by grace through faith - **Ephesians 2:8, 9**

"For by grace are ye saved through faith; and that not of yourselves: it is the gift of God: Not of works, lest any man should boast."

- That faith in Christ is necessary for salvation - **Galatians 3:26**

"For ye are all the children of God by faith in Christ Jesus."

- Baptism shows our faith in Christ and that we have made the decision to live like Christ which goes against infant baptism- **Romans 6:4**

"Therefore we are buried with him by baptism into death: that like as Christ was raised up from the dead by the glory of the Father, even so we also should walk in newness of life."

- That Jesus is the Son of God - **Romans 1:4**

"And declared to be the Son of God with power, according to the spirit of holiness, by the resurrection from the dead:"

- The death of Christ paid for our sins - **Galatians 6:14**

"But God forbid that I should glory, save in the cross of our Lord Jesus Christ, by whom the world is crucified unto me, and I unto the world."

I have mentioned these 6 things specifically for a reason. You will see later that the proponents of the Alexandrian manuscripts did not believe in those 6 very fundamental teachings from the Scriptures. More will be said about that later in this chapter.

They were called Christians first in Antioch, and, as I said before, there was a huge Christian influence there and a huge ministry of teaching and preaching of the Scriptures. There had to be not only the Old Testament copies there because these were Jews who came from Jerusalem because of the persecution, but there were possibly also many of the New Testament originals and copies. I say this because the Apostle Paul was an integral part of the church in Antioch and God used him, as you well know, to pen most of the New Testament. When Paul would travel on his evangelistic trips his custom, or manner was, "(he)…went in unto them (the people in the many cities he went to, to preach and teach the Scriptures to in their synagogues), and three sabbath days reasoned with them out of the scriptures, opening and alleging, that Christ must needs have suffered, and risen again from the dead; and that this Jesus, whom I preach unto you, is Christ." (Acts 17:2&3) No doubt as he taught them out of the Scriptures, since he was dealing mainly with the Jews, he was using the Old Testament which was what they all were more familiar with. But, as I said before, at Antioch it is a possibility that he also had much of the New Testament originals on hand or at least a first copy of them with him.

There is no doubt that Antioch was the "hot bed" of Christianity and that the most revered and trusted men were there working through the church of Antioch in the spreading of the Gospel, in the winning of people to Christ and in the planting of New Testament churches around the world which was near to them. What a great place to have been in the day.

Also, when we speak of the Antioch manuscripts, we are speaking of the manuscripts, which as I have mentioned before, which were originals or faithful copies of the originals. They had not been changed or altered as the Alexandrian manuscripts had been.

So, in those days there were faithful men who believed what the Bible taught and there were manuscripts which were either originals or faithful copies of originals in existence there in Antioch! From those men and manuscripts we have translations, as the men of Hampton Court said, "…they provided translations into the vulgar for their countrymen (from the Antioch line of manuscripts as we will see later), insomuch that most nations under heaven did shortly after their conversion hear Christ speaking unto them in their mother tongue, not by the voice of their minister only, but also by the written word translated." They continued to write that, "Every country that is under the sun is full of these words!" They then give an extensive list of the nations that had either a part of the Bible translated into the national language or the whole Bible so translated. Where did those translations come from? From which line of manuscripts did they come from and does it really matter? I earnestly contend that the translations mentioned were from the Antioch line of manuscripts and it matters! Why do I say that?

I say that because of the amount of full and partial manuscripts in existence of the Antioch line compared to the amount in existence from the Alexandrian line. In one source it

CHAPTER 14: ANTIOCH AND ALEXANDRIA

says there are 5,210 manuscripts of the Antioch line and only 45 of the Alexandrian line. These numbers seem to agree pretty closely with others I have read in other sources. There are also over 30,000 partial fragments which agree with the over 5,000 manuscripts of the Antioch line. Why is there so many more of the Antioch line than the Alexandrian? It has to do with which ones were used and which ones were not.

As I have stated before, there were many translations from the first century and on. The list of nations found in the letter to the readers from the translators of the King James Bible is quite impressive. It seems that where ever the Gospel went there was soon a translation into that language so the people did, "…hear Christ speaking unto them in their mother tongue, not by the voice of their minister only, but also by the written word translated." Another person once wrote that the natural result of missions was translation into the language of the people. All this agrees with Paul's writing in Corinthians about speaking in tongues.

1 Corinthians 14:4-13

> *"He that speaketh in an unknown tongue edifieth himself; but he that prophesieth edifieth the church. I would that ye all spake with tongues, but rather that ye prophesied: for greater is he that prophesieth than he that speaketh with tongues, except he interpret, that the church may receive edifying. Now, brethren, if I come unto you speaking with tongues, what shall I profit you, except I shall speak to you either by revelation, or by knowledge, or by prophesying, or by doctrine? And even things without life giving sound, whether pipe or harp, except they give a distinction in the sounds, how shall it be known what is piped or harped? For if the trumpet give an uncertain sound, who shall prepare himself to the battle? **So likewise ye, except ye utter by the tongue words***

easy to be understood, how shall it be known what is spoken? (Verse 9) for ye shall speak into the air. There are, it may be, so many kinds of voices in the world, and none of them is without signification. <u>**Therefore if I know not the meaning of the voice, I shall be unto him that speaketh a barbarian, and he that speaketh shall be a barbarian unto me. Even so ye, forasmuch as ye are zealous of spiritual gifts, seek that ye may excel to the edifying of the church. Wherefore let him that speaketh in an unknown tongue pray that he may interpret.*"*</u>

What good is a language in that which is not understood? There must be an interpreter. I have preached in different nations around the world and in almost every one of them I had an interpreter. Why? So the church could understand what was being said and be edified! Conversely, why do we need translations? I will deal with this in another chapter in the Translation section, but for now I will say we need translations for the same reason we need interpreters and those who can translate the Word of God into another language for the good of those who speak that language.

It would seem that the Antioch line of manuscripts were copied and recopied and used and re-used throughout the world to translate the Word of God from one language to another. One of the first translations was the Peshitta Bible for the Syrian people, (where was Antioch? – Syria) which was translated around 150 A.D. only about 50 years after John was inspired to write the Book of Revelation. Another was the Itala Bible around 157 A.D. And there were countless others throughout history starting at 150 all the way up to the King James Bible in 1611. They used the manuscripts that were available and accurate and descendants of the originals. My goodness there was also even a translation of the Hebrew into the Greek. Why? So those who spoke Greek could understand what was written in the Hebrew!

CHAPTER 14: ANTIOCH AND ALEXANDRIA

The point of all of this is to show you which line of manuscripts were used and therefore, preserved. The Antioch line of manuscripts were used over and over and therefore copied over and over for their use! All the while the Alexandrian line of manuscripts was lost for centuries! Unused and not copied over and over like the Antioch line was. In all of this the originals were copied and re-copied, used and re-used through the centuries giving us the over 5,000 manuscripts and 30,000 plus fragments. Thus PRESERVING the Word of God accurately and then translated accurately all of which is a process of the preservation of the Word of God! The King James Bible is an accurate translation of the preserved Word of God and the Antioch line of manuscripts are the foundational manuscripts upon which the King James Bible was translated.

But now, what about the Alexandrian line of manuscripts? I have a message I preach about a reason I use the Kings James Bible. A reason, not the only one, I use the King James Bible is because of ecclesiastical separation. Ecclesiastical separation says I will not yoke with unbelievers and with their false religions. There are many verses I could bring to the table but for now I want to simply show you some interesting things about the Alexandrian line of manuscripts.

The Alexandrian line of manuscripts does not have such men like Paul, Barnabas, Mark and the like associated with them. Instead they are associated with the like of Clement, Origen, Eusebius, Westcott and Hort and others of like thought.

Clement was a teacher in a catechetical school in Alexandria and accepted Greek philosophy and the Apocrypha as Divinely authoritative. He believed that salvation could be obtained by many different methods. Among these were baptism, faith and works and even faith alone. (It cannot be obtained by both faith and works and/or faith alone (Ephesians 2:8, 9). One of his students was a man named Origen.

Origen believed in "Universal salvation" meaning that eventually even Satan himself would end up getting saved. This is what he wrote on this,

> "God's first creation, BEFORE TIME, was a collectivity of souls. Of, these, all but one, the human soul of Jesus, fell away. In the end, however, ALL HUMANS AND EVERY SPIRIT, **<u>EVEN THE DEVIL WOULD BE SAVED RETURNING TO A STATE OF PURE MIND.</u>**"

This was and is such a false doctrine that even the Catholics pronounced him a heretic because of this teaching. In A.D. 553, the Council of Constantinople pronounced him a heretic saying,

> "WHOEVER SAYS OR THINKS THAT THE PUNISHMENT OF DEMONS AND THE WICKED SHALL NOT BE ETERNAL, LET HIM BE ANATHEMA."

He denied the Holy Spirits eternality, eternal punishment, the Bibles authority and salvation by grace and constantly used allegorizing of the Bible instead of believing it for what it says. There were other things he believed and wrote about.

> "What intellectual person can imagine that there was a first day then a second and third day- evening and morning –without the sun, moon and the stars…who is foolish enough to believe that, like a human gardener, God planted a garden in Eden…I cannot imagine that anyone will doubt that these details point SYMBOLICALLY to spiritual meanings, by using a historical narrative which did not literally happen. And who is so foolish as to suppose, as after the manner of an husbandman, God planted a garden in Eden, towards the east, and placed in it a tree of life,

CHAPTER 14: ANTIOCH AND ALEXANDRIA

> visible and palpable, so that one tasting of the fruit by the bodily teeth obtained life?"

Like Philo, Origen read Scripture allegorically as you can see above. He thought that since so many of the stories in the Bible were clearly false and even ridiculous, God's intention must have been that they NOT BE TAKEN LITERALLY. Then, one of the men who thought a lot about Origen and his teachings was a man named Eusebius another heretic.

These were the two main men behind the Alexandrian manuscripts. When you don't believe in salvation by grace and the Bible teaches it, then you must either change what you believe to agree with the Bible or change what the Bible says about it to agree with what you believe. This is exactly what happened. They changed the manuscripts omitting many words and even verses to agree with their teaching. May I give you just a few examples?

From a chart compiled showing the omissions and changes of versions of the Bible which were based on the Alexandrian line, the New International Version has omitted 5,219 words; the Revised Standard Version has omitted 6,985 words; the Living "Bible" has omitted 17,003 words. If we are supposed to live by EVERY WORD that proceeds out of the mouth of God, we had better have those words.

A very important question is asked in Acts 8:36 from a man who wanted to be baptized. It says, "And as they went on *their* way, they came unto a certain water: and the eunuch said, See, *here is* water; what doth hinder me to be baptized?" He wanted to be baptized and asked what was stopping him from being so. The answer is found in verse 37 which says, "And Philip said, If thou believest with all thine heart, thou mayest. And he answered and said, I believe that Jesus Christ is the Son of God." The Evangelist said the only thing stopping him from being baptized was whether or not he believed with all his heart what Phillip had just taught him from the Book of Isaiah about

Jesus being the Messiah, the Saviour of the world. The man's answer was, "...I believe that Jesus Christ is the Son of God." BOOM! The correct answer. Then because of the man's faith in Christ, guess what, HE WAS IMMEDIATELY BAPTIZED! (Verse 38) Faith in Christ ALWAYS COMES BEFORE BAPTISM! ALWAYS!

But in the following versions of the Bible based on the Alexandrian manuscripts, verse 37 is TOTALLY MISSING! New International Version, New American Standard Version, New King James "Bible," the Revised Standard Version, the New Revised Standard Version, the Living "Bible" and a popular one today the English Standard Version and many others. Why is such an important verse left out? They did not believe in salvation through Christ! They believed in baptismal regeneration! So, they had to cut it out of the manuscripts to change what God said making it agree with what they believed! Well, you say, that is only one example. Ok! Here are some more verses missing in those versions and others. Matthew 12:47; 17:21; 18:11; 21:44; 23:14; Mark 7:16; 9:44 & 46; 11:26; 15:28; 16:9-20; Luke 17:36, 22:43 & 44; 23:17; 24:12; 24:40; John 5:4; 7:53-8:11; Acts 15:34; 24:7 and 28:29!

Then there are words missing! Christ is missing 87 times in the New Revised Standard Version; Jesus is missing 292 times in the New International Version while hell is missing 41 times in the Revised Standard Version. Why? God is omitted 468 times in the New International Version! Why? Why are these verses and words missing? Because the Alexandrian line of manuscripts has been tampered with by religious unbelievers. Speaking of this, who else is a part of these manuscripts? I mentioned some above but first why these manuscripts were not even used or even in existence for over 1500 years? Why? Did not God promise that He would preserve His Word for every generation? Wouldn't God want people in the centuries following the second and third centuries to have His Word? Wouldn't there be other translations before 1582 when the Douay Version was translated? Why all of

CHAPTER 14: ANTIOCH AND ALEXANDRIA

a sudden were versions of the Bible not being translated until the middle to late 1800's? Just asking!

Dr. David Sorenson in his book <u>Touch Not the Unclean Thing</u> wrote on page 29 about the Alexandrian manuscripts commonly called the "Critical Text,"

> "Often overlooked by its proponents is taking the concept of the critical text to its logical conclusion. Therefore, consider this. If the critical text represents the superior and true text of the New Testament, then God allowed most of it to be hidden in the Vatican library and a Greek Orthodox monastery for approximately 1500 years. If that is the case, the Bible used by all the reformers and great Christian leaders prior to about 1900 A.D. was an inferior text. Moreover God used theological liberals and apostates in the nineteenth and twentieth centuries to cobble together the (so called) true text."

He further wrote on page 49,

> "The Received Text (Antioch manuscripts) is that lineage of manuscripts which trace back to the earliest days of *believing* (emphasis his), orthodox Christianity. These are the overwhelming majority of existing Greek manuscripts of the New Testament. Moreover, the majority of the manuscripts of the Received Text are so virtually unanimous in their consistency that the modern text critics have dismissed them as having a common source. They do. His name is the Holy Spirit." He then stated on pages 49 and 50, "By way of contrast, the chief Alexandrian manuscripts (which make up the essence of the critical text) are desperate in their readings. There is not consistency. They at times contradict each

other. Vaticanus and Sinaiticus alone show over **3,000 variants between themselves in just the Gospels alone!**" (Emphasis mine)

But let's look now at the two men who were instrumental at making the Alexandrian (Critical text) more popular.

A couple other men who were very involved in the Alexandrian line of manuscripts are the renowned Westcott and Hort. On a chart I have in my possession it says about these men, "They were both apostates. Westcott did not accept Genesis 1-3, the bodily resurrection of Christ or the miracles and literal coming of Christ and was partial to Romish ways. Hort did not accept the infallibility of Scriptures. He also favored Darwin's theory of evolution and both men did not believe in eternal punishment or Jesus vicarious atonement." (Providential Preservation of the Text of the New Testament)

These men were a part of the very liberal part of the Church of England and were known to dabble in séances and witchcraft. They believed that they could speak with the dead and practiced this in their organization known as the "Ghostly Guild" which they started and were a part of until after they began their work on the Critical text. And these are the men who revised the Greek in the Critical Text and are the champions of that line of manuscripts.

Ecclesiastical separation? You bet ya! I would much prefer to be associated with Paul than with Westcott. I would much rather read the writings of God through Paul, Matthew, John and all the other men God used to write His Word than to be associated and defend the works of Satanists, apostates and their material.

Antioch manuscripts instead of Alexandrian? Spot on!

Bibles that come from God preserved manuscripts instead of versions from human tampered with manuscripts. Absolutely!

CHAPTER 14: ANTIOCH AND ALEXANDRIA

King James Bible which came from the Received text (Antioch line) instead of the versions from the Critical text (Alexandrian line)? Without a doubt!

Do I believe in the Divine preservation of the inspired words of the Word of God? 100%!

Do I believe that the King James Bible is the perfectly preserved translation of the inspired Word of God? I have bet my future on it!

Do I use a version with words and verses missing and changed? Emphatically NO!

The order is Inspiration, Preservation and now Translation!

Chapter 15

Heretical Teachings About Preservation

Matthew 16:11 & 12

> *"How is it that ye do not understand that I spake it not to you concerning bread, that ye should beware of the leaven of the Pharisees and of the Sadducees? Then understood they how that he bade them not beware of the leaven of bread, but of the doctrine of the Pharisees and of the Sadducees."*

Whenever there is truth, there is also error. Truth is the Word of God! John 17:17 says, "Sanctify them through thy truth: thy word is truth." There are some who teach the Word of God incorrectly out of a lack of study personally but there are also some who teach it wrong out of a deceitful heart. Sadly, both kind of false teaching will have hearers, those who will hold to the teaching they hear out of innocence or just total willingness.

2 Timothy 4:1 - 4

> *"I charge thee therefore before God, and the Lord Jesus Christ, who shall judge the quick and the dead at his appearing and his kingdom; Preach the word; be instant in season, out of season; reprove, rebuke, exhort with all longsuffering and doctrine.* **For the time will come when they will not endure sound doctrine; but after their own lusts shall they heap to themselves teachers, having itching ears; And they shall turn away their ears from the truth, and shall be turned unto fables.*"*

CHAPTER 15: HERETICAL TEACHINGS

Why do our politicians believe any fable that comes down the road? Because they have turned from the truth and turned to fables. Why do some men preach heresy? They preach heresy because they have turned from the truth and turned to fables. Why are there people who listen to the politicians who believe lies and "preachers" who peddle heresy? Some do it out of ignorance, but sadly, some have turned from the truth to believe fables. Why do some believe in evolution? Because they have turned from truth to believe fables. Romans chapter one tells us of some of these people and WHY they believe and do what they please.

Romans 1:18-32

> *"For the wrath of God is revealed from heaven against all ungodliness and unrighteousness of men, who hold the truth in unrighteousness; Because that which may be known of God is manifest in them; for God hath shewed it unto them. For the invisible things of him from the creation of the world are clearly seen, being understood by the things that are made, even his eternal power and Godhead;* **so that they are without excuse:** *Because that, when they knew God, they glorified him not as God, neither were thankful; but became vain in their imaginations, and their foolish heart was darkened. Professing themselves to be wise, they became fools, And changed the glory of the uncorruptible God into an image made like to corruptible man, and to birds, and fourfooted beasts, and creeping things.*
>
> *Wherefore God also gave them up to uncleanness through the lusts of their own hearts, to dishonour their own bodies between themselves:* **Who changed the truth of God into a lie***, and worshipped and served the creature more than the Creator, who is blessed for ever. Amen.*

For this cause God gave them up unto vile affections: for even their women did change the natural use into that which is against nature: And likewise also the men, leaving the natural use of the woman, burned in their lust one toward another; men with men working that which is unseemly, and receiving in themselves that recompence of their error which was meet. And even as **they did not like to retain God in their knowledge**, *God gave them over to a reprobate mind, to do those things which are not convenient; Being filled with all unrighteousness, fornication, wickedness, covetousness, maliciousness; full of envy, murder, debate, deceit, malignity; whisperers, Backbiters,* **haters of God**, *despiteful, proud, boasters, inventors of evil things, disobedient to parents, Without understanding, covenantbreakers, without natural affection, implacable, unmerciful:* **Who knowing the judgment of God, that they which commit such things are worthy of death, not only do the same, but have pleasure in them that do them."**

Whether on purpose or out of ignorance; whether it is a decision which was made to turn from the truth or something that is done out of a lack of study and a looking to the teaching of men instead of comparing what men have taught to the Word of God, the problems that are a result of false teaching are horrendous. There are those who through itching ears heap to themselves teachers who will tell them what they want to hear. There are those who through ignorance believe what is said because of man worship and regurgitate what Dr. so and so taught. We ought to be more like the people of Berea who when they heard some new thing they looked to the Scriptures!

CHAPTER 15: HERETICAL TEACHINGS

Acts 17:11

"These were more noble than those in Thessalonica, in that they received the word with all readiness of mind, and searched the scriptures daily, whether those things were so."

There is a warning given in **2 Timothy 2:14** which states,

"Of these things put them in remembrance, charging them before the Lord that they strive not about words to no profit, but to the subverting of the hearers."

Words can and do "subvert the hearers! What is interesting about the word subvert in this verse is that the Greek word for it is the word, **"katastrophē!"** (And there are some who ridicule the looking up of words in the Bible in the Greek. Have they turned their ears from the truth)? Wrong words can cause a catastrophe in others' lives! Another interesting definition found in the Greek for the word subvert is the following from the Strong's Concordance...

G2692

καταστροφή

katastrophē

kat-as-trof-ay'

From G2690; an *overturn* ("catastrophe"), that is, **demolition; figuratively apostasy**: - overthrow, subverting.

What is taught MUST BE BIBLICAL! But how can we make sure it is Biblical? The answer is in the next verse in Second Timothy chapter two.

2 Timothy 2:15

> *"Study to shew thyself approved unto God, a workman that needeth not to be ashamed, rightly dividing the word of truth."*

The answer to words that subvert and makes apostates is STUDY! Study what? THE WORD OF TRUTH!

I have many books in my library which includes many commentaries. I read them when I have questions and consider what they might say but the Scriptures take the premiere place among them all and is my final authority. I have been taught by some great teachers, but if and when I hear false teaching I run to the Scriptures. I even have a very thick file folder or two of notes from when I would hear a teaching that I questioned I would write myself a note, go home and study it out to then find out if my understanding of that teaching was correct or if it was wrong.

From 2 Timothy 2:15 I have said the following for years. "If study causes us to rightly divide the word of truth, then a lack of study will cause us to wrongly divide the word of truth." The warning was about words that subvert the hearers. The solution is that we study the word of truth which then causes us to not be ashamed. Not be ashamed of what? Of using words or teachings which subvert the hearers. We have a great responsibility to make sure our words are used for the edifying of the hearers, not the subverting of the hearers. Now notice the next few verses please.

2 Timothy 2:16-18

> *"But shun profane and vain babblings: for they will increase unto more ungodliness. And their word will eat as doth a canker: of whom is Hymenaeus and Philetus;*
>
> *Who concerning the truth have erred, saying that the resurrection is past already; and overthrow the faith of some."*

Notice this in order from those verses…

CHAPTER 15: HERETICAL TEACHINGS

- Profane and vain babblings cause more ungodliness.
- Profane and vain babblings eat as doth a canker. This is one case where I not only looked into what the Greek word for "canker" is but also into a commentary. The result is a canker is like gangrene which is an infection that eats the flesh around it.
- Notice there are names connected with this false teaching and what it was.
- The false teaching was that the resurrection was past and then look at the result…
- It "(overthrew) the faith of some!

I have heard the false teachings about preservation and have seen the results! The faith of many have been overthrown in the King James Bible! They are now teaching things like the following…

- "God's Word is preserved, inspired Words; not just preserved Words!" Meaning it is the breath of God which is preserved keeping the words alive. (You will see this just below.)
- "If God's Words is not PRESERVED, INSPIRED WORDS, IT IS A DEAD WORD!" Meaning, if the breath of God is not still in the words, then it is dead!
- "God's Word can be accurate in its preservation, BUT WITHOUT INSPIRATION (God's breath in it) it is an embalmed Bible."
- "God's Word is either inspired (has God's breath IN IT) or expired."
- "If God's Word is preserved only, then when did it expire?"
- "If God's Word has expired, then we must go back to that date in order to have a LIVING written Word."
- "If the Word of God has expired, then Jesus expired on the same date."

These are all quotes from a "Bible study" I attended back in 2008 taken from the teachers own notes he handed out to everyone. In this same teaching was taught that, "Inspiration happens all the time!" He used 2 Timothy 3:16 to "prove" erroneously using the part which says, "IS given" which totally ignoring the Greek form of the word theopneustos and its meaning by saying, "The Scriptures are continually being inspired. It is still breathing, it is still being inspired." People left that room believing that the King James Bible is still being inspired today. But as I have pointed out in a previous chapter, the 'TOS' at the end of theopneustos is not in the linear or active but in the punctiliar or the passive meaning the Scriptures were GIVEN ONE TIME by inspiration, or by the breath of God as He spoke the words to the writers. Since then we have the preserved words of the Word of God which has been meticulously copied and accurately translated. Inspiration is not given, and given, and given, and given, it was GIVEN! Inspiration is not what God did to the Scriptures but how God GAVE the Scriptures!

Section 5
Translation

"But how shall men meditate in that which they cannot understand? How shall they understand that which is kept close in an unknown tongue?"

"…it is necessary to have translations in a readiness…Indeed without translation into the vulgar tongue, the unlearned are but like children at Jacob's well (which was deep) without a bucket or something to draw with…"

."…they provided translations into the vulgar for their countrymen, insomuch that most nations under heaven did shortly after their conversion hear Christ speak unto them in their mother tongue, not by the voice of their minister only, but also in the written word translated."

"Accurate translation of Scripture is a part of the process of the preservation of the already inspired Word given by God."

- Dr. Gary L. Mann –

Chapter 16

Why We Needed a Translation

What were the reasons for the translation of the King James Bible or any other Bible in other languages? Why did the man of Hampton Court and King James feel it necessary to have another translation of the Scriptures? Were they alone in this belief? What can we glean from the Scriptures themselves having to do with this topic? These and other questions will be answered both from the Bible and history and from the translators themselves. Some of this I have already mentioned but it is worth going through again to understand the need of translations and its process.

Before we get into some of this let me put down some definitions.

Translate – "To interpret; to render into another language; to express the sense of one language in the words of another." (Taken from Webster's 1828 dictionary.)

The Old Testament was translated into the Greek more than two hundred years before Christ. The Scriptures and now translated into most of the languages of Europe and Asia.

Translation – "That which is produced by turning into another language; a version."

What does it mean when the translators mention a "vulgar" language or tongue?

Vulgar – "The language used of practiced by the common people." In other words, the language everyone used and understands.

First things first. We know that the Scriptures were given, or breathed, by God. **2 Timothy 3:16** is clear on that. We also know from **Romans 15:4** that, *"For whatsoever things were*

CHAPTER 16: WHY WE NEEDED A TRANSLATION

written aforetime were written for our learning, that we through patience and comfort of the scriptures might have hope." Then in **John 5:39** we see we are to, *"Search the scriptures; for in them ye think ye have eternal life: and they are they which testify of me."* Next **in 1 Corinthians 10:11**, *"Now all these things happened unto them for ensamples: and they are written for our admonition, upon whom the ends of the world are come."* From these verses we learn the following...

• All Scripture is given by inspiration of God and is profitable,
• The Scriptures are given for our learning,
• We are to search the Scriptures which teach us about eternal life and about God and finally,
• All the things written in the Bible are for our example and admonition.

God wants His children to know some things about Him and how we are to get saved and live for Him. He has given us a Book telling us all we need to know and that Book is the Bible!

I have already mentioned some of this and will not go through it again but Peter, by inspiration, emphasized the importance of Scripture **in 2 Peter 1:13 through 21** when he wrote,

> *"Yea, I think it meet, as long as I am in this tabernacle, to stir you up by putting you in remembrance; Knowing that shortly I must put off this my tabernacle, even as our Lord Jesus Christ hath shewed me. Moreover I will endeavour that ye may be able after my decease to have these things always in remembrance. For we have not followed cunningly devised fables, when we made known unto you the power and coming of our Lord Jesus Christ, but were eyewitnesses of his majesty. For he received from God the Father honour and glory, when there came such a voice to him from*

> *the excellent glory, This is my beloved Son, in whom I am well pleased. And this voice which came from heaven we heard, when we were with him in the holy mount.* **We have also a more sure word of prophecy; whereunto ye do well that ye take heed, as unto a light that shineth in a dark place, until the day dawn, and the day star arise in your hearts: Knowing this first, that no prophecy of the scripture is of any private interpretation. For the prophecy came not in old time by the will of man: but holy men of God spake as they were moved by the Holy Ghost."**

Of all the things Peter saw while he was with Jesus and could tell them about, he said the Scriptures are a more sure word of prophecy and it is those sure words of prophecy that tell us the things about Jesus and the Father as given by the Spirit of God that we are to take heed to. THIS IS HOW IMPORTANT THE WORD OF GOD IS!

But why a TRANSLATION? What Biblical principle can we get from Scriptures to help us understand why we need a translation? The Biblical doctrine on languages and translation will help us in this area. What is the word "TONGUES" referring to?

Acts 2:1-11

> *"And when the day of Pentecost was fully come, they were all with one accord in one place. And suddenly there came a sound from heaven as of a rushing mighty wind, and it filled all the house where they were sitting. And there appeared unto them cloven tongues like as of fire, and it sat upon each of them. And they were all filled with the Holy Ghost, and began to speak with other tongues, as the Spirit gave them utterance. And there were dwelling at Jerusalem Jews, devout*

CHAPTER 16: WHY WE NEEDED A TRANSLATION

men, out of every nation under heaven. Now when this was noised abroad, the multitude came together, and were confounded, because that every man heard them speak in his own language. And they were all amazed and marvelled, saying one to another, Behold, are not all these which speak Galilaeans? And how hear we every man in our own tongue, wherein we were born? Parthians, and Medes, and Elamites, and the dwellers in Mesopotamia, and in Judaea, and Cappadocia, in Pontus, and Asia, Phrygia, and Pamphylia, in Egypt, and in the parts of Libya about Cyrene, and strangers of Rome, Jews and proselytes, Cretes and Arabians, we do hear them speak in our tongues the wonderful works of God."

We see the following...

- The 120 in the upper room began to speak in other "tongues."
- There were people in the area which were, "...out of every nation under heaven."
- There is a list of the "tongues" which were spoken by the disciples.
- The purpose for this miracle of the disciples in the upper room speaking in "tongues" was so the people could, "...(hear) the wonderful works of God."
- The direct result from them speaking in the "tongues" listed was that 3,000 people got saved and baptized that day!

What does "tongues" mean? The word "tongues" comes from the Greek word, "Glossa" which means, "the tongue; the LANGUAGE or dialect used by a particular group of people."

What does "language" mean? It comes from the Greek word, "dialectos" which means, "conversation, speech; the "tongue" or "language" peculiar to any people."

AND WHAT MARVEL!

What did Paul write about speaking in "tongues" or languages?
1 Corinthians 14:1-14

"Follow after charity, and desire spiritual gifts, but rather that ye may prophesy. For he that speaketh in an unknown tongue speaketh not unto men, but unto God: for no man understandeth him; howbeit in the spirit he speaketh mysteries. But he that prophesieth speaketh unto men to edification, and exhortation, and comfort. He that speaketh in an unknown tongue edifieth himself; but he that prophesieth edifieth the church. I would that ye all spake with tongues, but rather that ye prophesied: for greater is he that prophesieth than he that speaketh with tongues, except he interpret, that the church may receive edifying. Now, brethren, if I come unto you speaking with tongues, what shall I profit you, except I shall speak to you either by revelation, or by knowledge, or by prophesying, or by doctrine? And even things without life giving sound, whether pipe or harp, except they give a distinction in the sounds, how shall it be known what is piped or harped? For if the trumpet give an uncertain sound, who shall prepare himself to the battle? So likewise ye, except ye utter by the tongue words easy to be understood, how shall it be known what is spoken? for ye shall speak into the air. There are, it may be, so many kinds of voices in the world, and none of them is without signification. Therefore if I know not the meaning of the voice, I shall be unto him that speaketh a barbarian, and he that speaketh shall be a barbarian unto me. Even so ye, forasmuch as ye are zealous of spiritual gifts, seek that ye may excel to the edifying of the church. Wherefore let him that

CHAPTER 16: WHY WE NEEDED A TRANSLATION

speaketh in an unknown tongue pray that he may interpret. For if I pray in an unknown tongue, my spirit prayeth, but my understanding is unfruitful."

There were 6 basic lessons from these verses...

- The important thing is to be understood when we speak. (Verse 2 – "For he that speaketh in an *unknown* tongue speaketh not unto men, but unto God: for no man understandeth *him;* howbeit in the spirit he speaketh mysteries.")
- To be understood when we speak or read gives edification, exhortation and comfort. (Verse 3 – "But he that prophesieth speaketh unto men *to* edification, and exhortation, and comfort")
- It is more important for the church (the people gathered) to understand and be edified, or built up than it is for someone to be able to speak in an unknown language.
- If you speak in a language the people do not understand, there needs to be an interpreter.
- We must speak in words easy to be understood. (Verse 9)
- If you are not understood, what you are saying is worthless.

The same is true in what is read. If we do not speak the language a book is written in, I get absolutely nothing out of it. I would lay it aside and never touch it and therefore get nothing out of it.

So what were the reasons for the translation in 1604-1611? There were others reasons that I will not go into here but here were some of the basic ones then.

- They needed to counter the Roman Catholic translation that was being worked on at the time.
- There was a need for a translation for the people.

- The most important reason for a translation was the people.
- They wanted the Bible to be accessible and understandable to the common person.
- They realized the importance of the truth!

In my teaching about the 8 Points of the Great Commission are the following.

- We are to go into all the world.
- As we go into all the world we are to preach the Gospel.
- Those who trust Christ for salvation get baptized.
- We are to teach them all things which means we need people who know the material to be taught.
- We need materials IN THEIR LANGUAGE for them to learn from and study so they then can do the teaching.
- We need a place for them to come to (local church)
- That new local church then starts the process all over again.
- While we are doing all this God says He is with us!

While that is what I usually teach, as I sat here typing it I realized that not only do we need materials in their language for them to learn from and study, but the people doing the teaching either need to know the language or it must be interpreted, or translated, for the hearers while the teacher/preacher is speaking!

Somewhere I read the following, "The call for the Scriptures to be translated into several foreign languages is the natural outcome of early missionary activity." FOREIGN languages mean languages that are FOREIGN to us. This is why the missionary must learn the language of the nation he is going to otherwise he will be useless in the foreign mission field. And,

CHAPTER 16: WHY WE NEEDED A TRANSLATION

he must then work to supply materials in their language for them to learn from.

God in His eternal wisdom knew we would not understand Greek and Hebrew. Therefore He put it in the hearts of people before us to translate the Word of God from those languages into the English. We now have the perfectly preserved and accurately translated Word of God in the English language in the King James Bible! Thank God for those in the 1600's who knew the Hebrew, Greek and Latin who could TRANSLATE from those languages into the English so we the common man can read, understand and then preach and teach what God originally inspired.

Chapter 17

The Translators' Companies and Their Guidelines

For the most part the work of translating the Bible before 1611 was done by individuals. What makes me think this is not only that it is true, but that many of the Bible translations have the name of the man responsible for its translation. In thinking of this I think of Wycliffe, Tyndale, Coverdale, Erasmus and Luther. These were individuals who did their best in the work of translating the Scriptures from the Hebrew and Greek into English and German. But, the work of translating the King James Bible was done differently.

The "Men of Hampton Court" as I like to refer to them, used a totally different system of translating than did the men mentioned above. While the men above did the work mainly as individuals, the men of Hampton Court did their work corporately as individuals and in assigned companies. The companies were as follows…

The **Westminster company** had 10 men in it who were responsible to translate Genesis through 2 Kings then there was another 7 men in it who were responsible to translate Romans through Jude.

The next company was the **Oxford company** which had 7 men who worked on Isaiah through Malachi and another 8 men who translated Matthew through Acts and Revelation.

The third company was the **Cambridge company** which had 8 men who worked on 1 Chronicles through Ecclesiastes and another 7 who worked on the Apocrypha. There were a total of 47 men who were mainly responsible to work on the translating of the Hebrew and Greek into the English while also comparing their work with other existing translations including those of

CHAPTER 17: TRANSLATORS' COMPANIES & GUIDELINES

other languages, with the end result being the King James Bible of 1611.

There are many things that could be written about most of the men in the work of translation, but I will simply refer you to find and read, <u>Translators Revived</u> by Alexander McClure.

When they decided to go ahead with the project there were 15 rules that were implemented in their work going forward. They were the foundational rules that John Reynolds, who was in the Oxford company, has been credited with. These rules would apply to every man and company throughout the duration of the translation. They are being given three times in this book but they are important in each case and must be considered carefully and often. These rules were as follows:

- The ordinary Bible read in the church, commonly called the Bishops' Bible, to be followed, and as little altered as the truth of the original will admit.
- The names of the prophets and the holy writers, with the other names of the text, to be retained as nigh as may be, accordingly as they were vulgarly used.
- The old ecclesiastical words to be kept, viz., the word church not to be translated congregation etc.
- When a word hath divers significations, that to be kept which hath been most commonly used by the most of the ancient fathers, being agreeable to the propriety of the place and the analogy of the faith.
- The division of chapters to be altered either not at all, or as little as may be, if necessity so require.
- No marginal notes at all to be affixed, but only for the explanation of the Hebrew or Greek words which cannot, without some circumlocution, so briefly and fitly be expressed in the text.
- Such quotations of places to be marginally set down as shall serve for the fit reference of one Scripture to another.

- Every particular man or each company to take the same chapter or chapters; and having translated of amended them severally by himself where he thinker good, all to meet together, confer what they have done and agree for their parts what shall stand
- As any company hath dispatched any one book in this manner, they shall send it to the rest to be considered of seriously and judiciously, for his Majesty is very careful in this point.
- If any company, upon review of the book so sent, doubt of differ upon any place, to send them word thereof, note the place, and withal send the reasons; to which if they consent not, the difference to be compounded at the general meeting, which is to be of the chief persons of each company at the end of the work.
- When any place of special obscurity is doubted of, letters to be directed by authority to send to any learned man in the land for his judgment of such a place.
- Letters to be sent from every bishop to the rest of his clergy, admonishing them of this translation in hand, and to move and charge as many as being skillful in the tongues, and having taken pains in the kind, to send his particular observations to the company at Westminster, Cambridge, or Oxford.
- The director of each company to be the Dean of Westminster, and Chester for that place, and the king's professors in the Hebrew or Greek in either university.
- These translations to be used when they agree better with the text than the Bishop's Bible: Tyndale, Matthew's, Coverdale's, Whitchurch's, Geneva.
- Besides the said directors before mentioned, three of four of the most ancient and grave divines in either of the universities, not employed in translating, to be assigned by the Vice-Chancellor upon conference with the rest of the Heads to be overseers of the translations, as

CHAPTER 17: TRANSLATORS' COMPANIES & GUIDELINES

well Hebrew as Greek, for the better observation of the fourth rule specified.

Much more will be written later about their work and the rules. This chapter is simply an informational one giving you some background into the Men of Hampton Court and the rules that guided them through the translation process.

Chapter 18

𝔇ynamic and 𝔉ormal 𝔈quivalence

2 Peter 1:19-21

> "We have also a more sure word of prophecy; whereunto ye do well that ye take heed, as unto a light that shineth in a dark place, until the day dawn, and the day star arise in your hearts: Knowing this first, that no prophecy of the scripture is of any private interpretation. For the prophecy came not in old time by the will of man: but holy men of God spake as they were moved by the Holy Ghost."

From the men of Hampton Court to the readers,

"We desire that the Scriptures may speak like itself, as in the language of Canaan, that it may be understood even of the very vulgar."

I was preaching and teaching at a King James Bible Research Council in Michigan one year when I was asked to be on the advisory board of the Council. I accepted and considered it an honor. My wife was there when Dr. Brown asked me if I would accept and she was thrilled and shocked that I would be asked to be a part of this group when she considered the caliber of men who are involved in it. I was just as shocked.

On my way home from that meeting, I began to wonder what I could do to be a positive contributor to this group of men. I thought of some of the men who were involved and what they have done and taught. I thought of Dr. Brown, the founder of the group, with his Ph.D. in history. I then thought of Dr. Sorenson, who, of all things, has written a commentary on the Bible and many other very helpful books on the Bible and is a man of powerful intellect. Then there is Dr. Phil Stringer who has written

CHAPTER 18: DYNAMIC & FORMAL EQUIVALENCE

many books including books on American History and who teaches all sorts of things all over the world. I then thought of Dr. Lance Ketchum who is a prolific writer and also a man with a deep understanding of the Bible and tremendous speaker. When I got home, I emailed Dr. Brown and asked what area I could possibly fill and what could I teach that others have not. His answer was swift. He emailed me back and said to study on Dynamic and Formal Equivalence. I promptly answered him and said I would, as soon as I figured out what it was! Well, I have studied on it and now have some material on it that is very relevant to our study of the translation of the Bible because Dynamic and Formal Equivalency are two very diametrically opposed methods of translation work.

In his book The Sinfulness of Sin, Ralph Venning, a Puritan from the mid 1600's said,

> "(Because of sin) man has become so sottish and brutish that he lives by his senses."

This is important to remember when speaking of Dynamic Equivalency.

As I said before, dynamic and formal equivalency are opposing methods of translation and interpretation of Scripture. The terms dynamic and formal equivalence were coined, as far as I have found, by a man named Eugene Nida though he was not the first person to use these forms of translation and interpretation. Mr. Nida was for more than thirty years the Executive Secretary of the Translations Department of the American Bible Society from 1946 until 1980. The true originator of dynamic equivalence is Satan himself! God said in **Genesis 2:16 & 17,**

> "And the LORD God commanded the man, saying, Of every tree of the garden thou mayest freely eat: But of the tree of the knowledge of good and evil, thou shalt not eat of it: for in the day that thou eatest thereof thou shalt surely die."

Satan, who did not agree with God, said in his conversation with Eve in **Genesis 3:1-5,**

> *"Now the serpent was more subtil than any beast of the field which the LORD God had made. And he said unto the woman,* **Yea, hath God said, Ye shall not eat of every tree of the garden?** *And the woman said unto the serpent, We may eat of the fruit of the trees of the garden: But of the fruit of the tree which is in the midst of the garden, God hath said, Ye shall not eat of it, neither shall ye touch it, lest ye die. And the serpent said unto the woman,* **Ye shall not surely die: For God doth know that in the day ye eat thereof, then your eyes shall be opened, and ye shall be as gods, knowing good and evil."**

In order for Satan to get Eve to disobey what God said, he had to <u>change the words of God and put it in his own words.</u> In other words, this is the first time a form of dynamic equivalence took place. Instead of quoting God word for word (formal equivalence), he gave it another sense, one that agreed with his own sense or agenda which is exactly what dynamic equivalence is.

Dynamic equivalence is not a word for word method of translation, but, according to Nida himself from his book <u>The Theory and Practice of Translation</u> we see the following, "…Dynamic equivalence is the quality of a translation in which the message of the original text has been so transported into the receptor language that the response of the receptors is essentially like that of the original receptors." That all sounds good on face value, but the problem is that a person who uses the dynamic equivalency method of translation in translating the Bible, "…(it) becomes very difficult for a translator to decode the whole text…literally; THEREFORE HE TAKES THE HELP OF HIS OWN VIEW AND ENDEAVORS TO TRANSLATE

CHAPTER 18: DYNAMIC & FORMAL EQUIVALENCE

ACCORDINGLY." Thus you do not have a translation from God's point of view but from that of the translator.

If while the translator us trying to translate from one language to another and his translation does not convey what he thinks the source is trying to convey, he will then TAKE LIBERTIES AND ACTUALLY STOP WORD FOR WORD TRANSLATION AND GO FOR SENSE TO SENSE TRANSLATION! **This form of translation (D.E.) is not then a translation but a mutation of the original source!** Remember what Venning said, "Because of sin, man lives by sense!

This form of translation agrees with Thomas Paine who said, "My own mind is my own church. Our observation that the Bible is a difficult book to those who are outside the church does not sit well with many people these days. On the contrary, they say the Bible is really quite simple; it is all a matter of translation. The old literal method of translation, which makes for such hard reading, is to blame. But if we will only put the Bible in easier more idiomatic English, it will need no explanation. People who are unfamiliar with church jargon might then read and understand it with ease."

This is the basic presupposition of the method of translation called dynamic equivalence. The cry for more "Bibles" comes from people's disagreement with what God said and how He said it. They say that we must have an "easier to read and understand" version. I say that the King James Bible is very easy to read and understand IF YOU ARE BORN OF THE SPIRIT! **2 Corinthians 2:12-16** teaches,

"Furthermore, when I came to Troas to preach Christ's gospel, and a door was opened unto me of the Lord, I had no rest in my spirit, because I found not Titus my brother: but taking my leave of

them, I went from thence into Macedonia. Now thanks be unto God, which always causeth us to triumph in Christ, and maketh manifest the savour of his knowledge by us in every place. For we are unto God a sweet savour of Christ, in them that are saved, and in them that perish: To the one we are the savour of death unto death; and to the other the savour of life unto life. And who is sufficient for these things? For we are not as many, which corrupt the word of God: but as of sincerity, but as of God, in the sight of God speak we in Christ."

The problem of understanding the Bible is not in the translation but in a person's salvation! This is why a person MUST be born again. If we have the Spirit of God in our lives, Who comes into our lives at salvation, then, and only then, can we really understand the Bible. This is also why the Word of God was given to Holy men of old and they wrote as the SAME Spirit of God moved them. More will be said about this later.

Dynamic equivalence eschews "STRICT ADHERENCE TO THE GRAMMATICAL STRUCTURE OF THE ORIGINAL TEXT IN FAVOR OF A MORE "NATURAL" RENDERING." (According to the translators) in the target language, or the language it is being translated into. Dynamic equivalence it sometimes used when the readability of the translation is more important than the preservation of original grammatical structure. We have the inspired words of the Word of God today because of the meticulous, letter for letter copying of the scribes and the careful word for word translation of the Word of God from the original languages into the target languages by the translators. Dynamic equivalence ignores what God said and how He said it and when you change what He said, you therefore change the sense of what He said. IF you translate from the original into the target language word for word, you then get the accurate sense of what God said and means.

CHAPTER 18: DYNAMIC & FORMAL EQUIVALENCE

Using the dynamic equivalence method of translation makes the translator,

> "... (More) free from the grammatical forms of the original language..." so the translator is, "...likely to EXCEED THE BOUNDS OF AN ACCURATE TRANSLATION, in an effort to speak naturally..."

Translators who use the dynamic equivalent method in their attempt to be precise in the translation, "...are more capable of being precisely wrong!"

In another place is this,

> "Dynamic equivalence attempts to convey the THOUGHT expressed in the source text using equivalent expressions from a contemporary language..."

Therefore justifying modern "Bibles" using slang and the vernacular of today. (As seen in the Ebonic "Bible")

Formal equivalence on the other hand, is the method of translation which translates from the original source in a word for word, not a sense for sense, manner. Since the Bible is such an important book it deserves our utmost care in translation. How then can we be careless with the words of the Word?

In writing about formal equivalence a man said, "For detailed, in depth study into what God's Word teaches, however, the exactness of a formal equivalence translation is the best. Formal equivalence focuses attention on the message itself in both form and content." I believe that if you translate in a word for word way that you will also get the sense of the original meaning.

Interesting to note, the King James Bible is translated in the formal equivalence manner from the Antioch or Received Text. The Revised andAmerican Standard versions and the New King James also use the formal equivalence method. The problem here is the fact that those versions original source are the corrupted, Critical, Alexandrian texts. To make some comparisons let's look at the following…

- King James Bible uses good translators, formal equivalence and the Received or Antioch text.
- The others use bad translators, poor translation techniques and corrupted texts.
- The King James Bible lifts up pure doctrine while the others push such doctrines as evolution, rationalism, liberalism and higher criticism.
- The King James is translated word for word while the others are sense for sense.

I am going to take all this a step further.

Dynamic inspiration is where God would give men the words to write and they wrote them down in their own words as they thought it would make sense in their time.

Dynamic preservation would be where the scribes whose job it was to accurately copy the manuscript before them would change letters and words to fit their own ideology. This actually happened and is why we have corrupted manuscripts in existence today. Accurate manuscripts would be word for word, yea, letter for letter copying which is where we would place the Textus Receptus.

Dynamic exposition involves the preaching of the Word being done as we see it instead of how God sees things. We have been taught that a text taken out of its context makes it a pretext. A pretext is a pretense of false appearance. We are to study to rightly divide God's Word but dynamic exposition would be to take what God said and give it a different sense or meaning in agreement with our own thoughts.

Anytime people are given the freedom to translate using contemporary sense instead of word for word translating methods will change what God has said! The cry for an "understandable

CHAPTER 18: DYNAMIC & FORMAL EQUIVALENCE

Bible" is really very easily read as a slap in the face of God Almighty. When you actually translate Scripture using the formal equivalence method as the men of Hampton Court did, you not only translate the words of God but you also bring out the sense which He intended. The men of Hampton Court used as their primary method of translation the word for word method now called formal equivalency. They did not leave us with a question mark about what God said as the versions leave in the hearts of their readers. We have the Word of God!

Chapter 19

𝔗𝔥𝔢 𝔗𝔯𝔞𝔫𝔰𝔩𝔞𝔱𝔬𝔯𝔰

From the men of Hampton Court to the readers,

"And this is the word of God which we translate."

Much of the discussion about the inspiration of the Bible centers around whether or not the men of Hampton Court were inspired like Moses through the Apostle John were. As I have stated many times the difference between Moses and the men of Hampton Court is a blank sheet of paper. Moses had no idea what God was going to tell him to write, but then when God spoke the words He wanted Moses to write Moses obeyed. This was the process of inspiration. Through the process of time those parchments through use and age would fall apart but before they did they were copied by scribe's letter for letter. This is the process of preservation. Copies of copies eventually ended up in the hands of men like the men of Hampton Court who took those manuscripts and translated them into other languages which, of course, is the work of translation. But the men of Hampton Court did not start out with blank pages; they had what had been preserved in the manuscripts and the Textus Receptus.

There are those like Peter Ruckman and Gail Riplinger and their followers who espouse dual and even triple inspiration which I wrote about earlier. Then there are others, who in order to get away from the dual and triple inspiration teaching, have come up with what is called continuous inspiration which has also been dealt with in another chapter. Then men like Peter Ruckman also teach that the English corrects the Greek and Hebrew, and the King James Bible is a "new revelation from God to the translators of the 1611 Authorized Version" He also states,

"…the King James Version alone is the inspired Word of God."

CHAPTER 19: THE TRANSLATORS

Well, I guess no one had it then before 1611?! He went on to teach, "(one of the things to be emphasized) the absolute insanity of translating ANY Greek text literally, word for word, (where have we heard that before?) in order to give the reader THE WORDS God wants him to have in another language." He goes on later and wrote, "The King James Bible...often contains revelations of the truth that EVIDENTLY CANNOT BE FOUND IN ANY GREEK TEXT! So much for God giving men the Word of God in the Greek. Evidently God did not realize He was not giving man all we needed when He spoke the Word of God to Paul and the others. I guess we really didn't, according to Ruckman, have the Word of God until 1611. I digress back to the men of Hampton Court.

This chapter is going to deal specifically with the translators OWN WORDS to help and to settle whether or not they were inspired. I will begin with the Introduction to the Bible in the front of probably every King James Bible. It says,

The

Holy Bible

Containing the

Old and New Testaments

Translated out of the original tongues

And with the former translations

Diligently compared and revised by

His Majesty's Special Command

Notice the words, TRANSLATED, COMPARED AND REVISED! That doesn't sound like being inspired to me! Just a thought!

In their letter to the readers they emphasized the following, "That out of the original sacred tongues (Hebrew,

Aramaic and Greek)...there should be one more exact TRANSLATION of the Holy Scriptures into the English tongue..." They understood that what they were doing was TRANSLATING the words of God from the ORIGINAL SACRED TONGUES, into the English tongue.

Later in their letter to the readers it states, "If truth be to be tried by these tongues (Hebrew and Greek), then whence should a translation be made, but out of them? These tongues therefore (the Scriptures, we say, in those tongues) we set before us to TRANSLATE being the tongues wherein God was pleased to speak to His church by the Prophets and Apostles." Notice they called the Hebrew and Greek...

- The Scriptures in those tongues
- That was what they were going to use as their main foundation for translation,
- The languages God spoke through the Prophets and Apostles speaking about the inspiration of the Scriptures?

Some today deny that the Hebrew and Greek were even the languages God used to speak to the Prophets and Apostles and they deny that they were the Scriptures. The men of Hampton Court were not confused by this.

They understood their work was different from the Prophets and Apostles who were inspired while the work they did was TRANSLATION! They understood their work was translation which, along with the amount of material they had to translate and the great amount of resources at hand is one reason why it took so long to do their work. Plus, have you ever tried to get things done when you had 46 or so others working on the same thing. Amazing!

In the last part of their written statement mentioned in the paragraph above they wrote, "These tongues therefore (the Scriptures, we say, in those tongues) we set before us to TRANSLATE being the tongues wherein God was pleased to

CHAPTER 19: THE TRANSLATORS

speak to His church by the Prophets and Apostles." They differentiated, or made a difference, between what they did in comparison to what the Prophets and Apostles did. The work of the men of Hampton Court was that of TRANSLATION while the method God used to, "...speak to His church by the Prophets and Apostles," was INSPIRATION!

In a recent discussion on the internet I had with a man about the original languages and the King James Bible, I mentioned the many churches and Bible colleges who's Doctrinal Statements says something about the King James Bible being DERIVED from the Hebrew and Greek. He believes that the English in the King James Bible corrects those languages because, according to him, no preserved Hebrew or Greek manuscripts in existence. When I then pointed out that the King James Bible was DERIVED from the Hebrew and Greek, which means the English TRANSLATION comes from those languages, he totally rejected that because he believes the men of Hampton Court were inspired and that they did not need those languages especially, according to him, those are dead languages now anyhow. By the way, he teaches Bible through an internet "Bible College," whose Bible authority was a woman! In a phone conversation with the President of that online Bible College I asked why they could not find a man who was a preacher who was their Bible authority. There was no answer.

I wrote back to the Bible teacher tongue in cheek, "Most churches doctrinal statements have that the King James Bible is derived from the Hebrew and Greek (the Hebrew Masoretic and the Textus Receptus). So those churches and colleges then have a wrong doctrinal statement." His answer was, "Yes, it would be a good thing for churches to be taught the truth and to then clarify their doctrinal statement." My answer was, "They don't need fixing, they are already correct in their doctrinal statement," which the translators themselves would agree with according to their own statements.

The men of Hampton Court then wrote under the heading of Translations Necessary, "...it is necessary to have translation in a readiness. Translation it is that openeth the window, to let in the light; that breakes the shell, that we may eat the kernel. That putteth aside the curtain, that we may look into the most holy place; that removeth the cover of the well, by which the flocks of Laban were watered. Indeed without translation into the vulgar tongue, the unlearned are but like children at Jacob's well (which was deep) without a bucket or something to draw with: or as that person mentioned by Esay, to whom when a sealed book was delivered with this message, Read this, I pray thee, he was fain to make this answer, I cannot, for it is sealed." Also later they wrote, "And this is the word of God which we translate." They understood their part in the work they were doing, it was the work of Translation.

They also understood who was inspired and who was not. Earlier I copied this from the letter, "These tongues therefore (the Scriptures, we say, in those tongues) we set before us to TRANSLATE being the tongues wherein God was pleased to speak to His church by the Prophets and Apostles." Enough comments were made then to get the point; they knew that they were not inspired as were the Prophets and Apostles. In speaking about the 70 who translated the Septuagint they wrote, "...the seventy were interpreters, they were not prophets." They again, knew that the work of translation was not the work of inspiration. Earlier in the letter they wrote quoting Justin Martyr, "We must know by all means (saith he) that it is not lawful (or possible) to learn (anything) of God or of right piety, save only that of the Prophets, who teach us by Divine inspiration." They understood what inspiration was and who WAS inspired, AND THEY NEVER CLAIMED TO HAVE BEEN INSPIRED!

Of the seven year process of their in translating the Bible from the original languages they wrote in their letter to the King, "...**out of the Original Sacred Tongues** (they were DERIVED FROM – note mine), together with **comparing** of the labours, both in our own, and other foreign languages, of many worthy men who went before us, there should be one more **_exact translation_** of the holy Scriptures into the English Tongue..." They not only used the Original tongues (Hebrew, Aramaic and Greek) but many others also and they compared their labours with other men's translations in other languages. This does not sound like inspiration! Theirs was the work of translation...AND THEY KNEW IT AND WERE NOT ASHAMED OF THEIR PART OF TRANSLATION! THEY NEVER COMPARED THEMSELVES OR THEIR WORK WITH THE INSPIRATION OF THE PROPHETS AND APOSTLES! NEVER!

I have to conclude by their own testimony, that what the men of Hampton Court accomplished was not through the work of God through inspiration as some believe, but, by their own words it was done by the laborious process of TRANSLATION!

Chapter 20

More Reasons the Men of Hampton Court Were Not Inspired

All of this is taken directly from the notes of a message I taught at a National King James Bible Research Conference.

2 Timothy 3:16, 17

> *All scripture is given by inspiration of God, and is profitable for doctrine, for reproof, for correction, for instruction in righteousness:*
>
> *That the man of God may be perfect, throughly furnished unto all good works.*

Deuteronomy 8:3

> *And he humbled thee, and suffered thee to hunger, and fed thee with manna, which thou knewest not, neither did thy fathers know; that he might make thee know that man doth not live by bread only, but by every word that proceedeth out of the mouth of the LORD doth man live.*

Matthew 4:4

> *But he answered and said, It is written, Man shall not live by bread alone, but by every word that proceedeth out of the mouth of God.*

A study on "Inspiration" answering the question, "Were the Translators of the King James Bible inspired?"

My topic is, are translations inspired? Specifically, I want to look at the King James Bible and look at the men of Hampton Court who did the work of translation

CHAPTER 20: THE MEN OF HAMPTON COURT NOT INSPIRED

We must first understand what inspiration is.

- I could talk for days on what is being taught as inspiration which is not correct. But, for a good teaching on that go to the King James Bible Research Council website and find the article on <u>What Inspiration is Not!</u>
- 2 Timothy 3:16 – *"All scripture is given by inspiration of God, and is profitable for doctrine, for reproof, for correction, for instruction in righteousness:"*
- This verse is not talking about what God did to the Scriptures but how God GAVE the Scriptures.
- Theopneustos = God-breathed; inspiration – the English words are not based on English but on the Latin. The "spir" comes from the Latin "spirare" which means to breathe.

In 2008 when the debate started all over again, I wrote my pastor telling him where I stood on the topic. I wrote, "First of all I believe that, 'All scripture *is* given by inspiration of God,' this took place when, "…holy men of God spake as they were moved by the Holy Ghost…' (2 Peter 1:21) This refers to all the men who were used of God to write the complete canon of Scripture from Genesis to Revelation. As the Scriptures clearly state, "Knowing this first, that no prophecy of the Scripture is of any private interpretation. For the prophecy came not in old time by the will of man; but holy men of God spake as they were moved by the Holy Ghost.' (2 Peter 1:20, 21) This is speaking about the inspiration not the translation.

Secondly, I believe that since the inspiration of the Scriptures to those "holy men of God," that the Word of God has been Divinely preserved in its' entirety so that we have the preserved Word of God today in the English language, and in some other languages, as it was translated into the English language and we have the infallible, inerrant and preserved Word of God in the King James Bible.

This preservation took place through thousands of years of copying the manuscripts by who knows how many different people including scribes whose job it was to carefully and meticulously copy manuscripts letter by letter and word for word. The word 'preserve' from the Webster's 1828 dictionary means, 'To save from decay; to keep in a sound state; To keep or defend from corruption' There are more definitions included in the Webster's but these best describe what took place as God in His Sovereignty through Divine providence preserved His word so we would have His word today in an accurate, infallible and complete record of the inspired Word of God in our language.

If by the phrase, the King James Bible is inspired you mean that the men who translated the Word of God from the Hebrew and Greek to the English were inspired, I do not believe that. The inspiration took place to the holy men of God who spake as the Holy Ghost moved them and were preserved from corruption since then. The translators never claimed inspiration and nowhere in the Scriptures does God attribute that to them or to the scribes. If by the phrase the King James Bible is inspired you mean that the infallible, inerrant and preserved Word of God is there in its entirety and accurately , then I do believe that but I think it would be better to say the King James Bible is the preserved Word of God.

Yes, I believe that we have today in the King James Bible, which is a translation from the Hebrew and Greek into the English, the infallible, inerrant and preserved Word of God."

Other quotes:

From the King James Bible Research Council website.

> "We believe the Holy Scripture, the 66 canonical books of the Old and New Testaments, are given by inspiration of God, and are able to make men wise unto salvation through faith which is in Christ Jesus."

CHAPTER 20: THE MEN OF HAMPTON COURT NOT INSPIRED

From a Baptist College in the south.

"We believe the Holy Bible was written by men supernaturally inspired; that it has truth for its matter without any admixture of error; that it is and shall remain to the end of the age the only complete and final revelation of the will of God to man; and that it is the true center of Christian union and the supreme standard by which all human conduct, creeds, and opinions should be tried.

We believe the Authorized (King James) Version, Old and New Testaments, is the Word of God kept intact for English-speaking peoples by way of God's divine providence and work of preservation; and that the Authorized Version translators were not "inspired," but were merely God's instruments used to preserve His words for English-speaking peoples.

By Holy Bible we mean that collection of sixty-six books, from Genesis to Revelation, which, as originally written and providentially preserved, does not only contain and convey the Word of God, but is the very Word of God.

By inspiration we mean that the books of the Bible were written by holy men of God as they were moved by the Holy Ghost in such a definite way that their writings were supernaturally and verbally inspired and free from error, as no other writings have ever been or ever will be inspired.

By providentially preserved we mean that God through the ages has, in His divine providence, preserved the very words that He inspired; that the Hebrew Old Testament text, as found in the Traditional Masoretic Text, and the

> Greek New Testament text, as found in the Textus Receptus, are indeed the products of God's providential preservation and are altogether the complete, preserved, inerrant Word of God.
>
> We therefore believe and require that the Authorized Version (King James Version) be the only English version used and or endorsed by the staff, faculty, and student body of this college.

From a Baptist periodical.

> "**WE BELIEVE** the Bible, the Scriptures of the Old Testament and the New Testament, preserved for us in the Masoretic text (Old Testament) Textus Receptus (New Testament) and in the King James Bible, is verbally and plenarily inspired of God. It is the inspired, inerrant, infallible, and altogether authentic, accurate and authoritative Word of God, therefore the supreme and final authority in all things (II Tim. 3:16-17; II Peter 1:21; Rev. 22:18-19)."

H.D. Williams –

> "Inspiration is the miracle whereby the words of the Hebrew, Aramaic and Greek were God breathed and once delivered using holy men of God and their vocabulary, who perfectly recorded them once as they were moved along by the Holy Ghost in such a way that all the words are infallible, and inerrant in the 66 books of the canon of Scripture."

Dr. Sorenson –

> "The word translated as inspiration is the (Greek word) theopneustos. Any student of Scripture knows that the word means God-breathed. But what does God- breathed mean? I submit that

CHAPTER 20: THE MEN OF HAMPTON COURT NOT INSPIRED

> God-breathed is a reference to being God spoken. Every time we speak, we breathe out words. So did God when He gave His word to holy men of God."

Dr. Sorenson –

> "It is significant to notice that it is the Scriptures which are inspired...what they wrote were words- the basic vehicle of thought created by God Himself...as any serious student of the Bible knows, the term theopneustos is comprised of two smaller words, theo and pneustos which literally means "God breathed."...then the Bible is a God spoken book." (MY NOTE – The "tos at the end when connected with theos is in the passive tense, not the active, meaning it is done.)

Lockyer from his work including <u>All the Doctrines of the Bible</u> on pages 7 & 8.

> "The particular word used by Paul (theopneustos) means God-breathed. That is, God Himself or through the Holy Spirit, TOLD THE WRITERS OF THE BIBLE THE VERY THINGS TO WRITE."

John R. Rice in his book <u>Our God Breathed Book the Bible</u> on page 49,

> "...the meaning of the original Greek theopneustos ...is literally God-breathed. All Scripture is God-breathed, that is, THE SCRIPTURE ITSELF IS BREATHED OUT FROM GOD. GOD IS ITS ORIGIN, THE MIRACLE OF THE SCRIPTURE CAME DIRECTLY FROM GOD.

Shelton Smith from his work entitled <u>The Book We Call the Bible</u>,

> "God-breathed means that actual words of Scripture are the fruit of His very own breath. In this context of creating Scripture it does not just mean that God exuded His influence on it, BUT IT MEANS THAT HE BREATHED OT WORDS...HE GAVE EACH OF THE WRITERS HIS VERY OWN WORDS!"

How about the translators themselves from their letter to the readers in the front of many of the King James Bibles?

> "If truth be to be tried by these things (original Hebrew and Greek), then whence should a translation be made, but out of them. These tongues therefore (the Scriptures, we say, in those tongues) WE SET BEFORE US TO TRANSLATE BEING THE TONGUES WHEREIN GOD WAS PLEASED TO SPEAK TO HIS CHURCH BY HIS PROPHETS AND APOSTLES."

(They knew their job was to translate what had already been inspired. – Gary Mann)

> "And what marvel? The original thereof being from heaven, not from earth; the author being God, not man; the indictor, the Holy Spirit, not the wit of the Apostles and Prophets; the penmen, such as were sanctified from the womb, and endued with the principle portion of God's Spirit..."

(They understood the process of inspiration and that they were not a part of it. – Gary Mann)

How about some Bible Verses?

Exodus 9:1

> **Then the LORD said unto Moses**, *Go in unto Pharaoh, and tell him,* **Thus saith the LORD God**

CHAPTER 20: THE MEN OF HAMPTON COURT NOT INSPIRED

of the Hebrews, Let my people go, that they may serve me.

Exodus 24:4

***And Moses wrote all the words of the LORD**, and rose up early in the morning, and builded an altar under the hill, and twelve pillars, according to the twelve tribes of Israel.*

Exodus 34:27

And the LORD said unto Moses, Write thou these words: for after the tenor of these words I have made a covenant with thee and with Israel.

1 Kings 12:22-24

***But the word of God came unto Shemaiah the man of God, saying, Speak** unto Rehoboam, the son of Solomon, king of Judah, and unto all the house of Judah and Benjamin, and to the remnant of the people, **saying, Thus saith the LORD**, Ye shall not go up, nor fight against your brethren the children of Israel: return every man to his house; for this thing is from me. They hearkened therefore to the word of the LORD, and returned to depart, according to the word of the LORD.*

Kings 21:17-19

***And the word of the LORD came to Elijah the Tishbite, saying,** Arise, go down to meet Ahab king of Israel, which is in Samaria: behold, he is in the vineyard of Naboth, whither he is gone down to possess it. **And thou shalt speak unto him, saying, Thus saith the LORD**, Hast thou killed, and also taken possession? **And thou shalt speak unto him, saying, Thus saith the LORD**, In the place where dogs licked the blood of Naboth shall dogs lick thy blood, even thine.*

Psalm 68:11

The Lord gave the word: *great was the company of those that published it.*

Psalm 119:88

Quicken me after thy lovingkindness; so shall I keep the testimony of thy mouth.

Psalm 138:4

All the kings of the earth shall praise thee, O LORD, **when they hear the words of thy mouth.**

Isaiah 55:11

So shall my word be that goeth forth out of my mouth: *it shall not return unto me void, but it shall accomplish that which I please, and it shall prosper in the thing whereto I sent it.*

Jeremiah 1:4

Then the word of the LORD came unto me, saying,

Ezekiel 2:2

And the spirit entered into me when he spake unto me, and set me upon my feet, that I heard him that spake unto me.

Ezekiel 11:5

And the Spirit of the LORD fell upon me, and said unto me, Speak; Thus saith the LORD; *Thus have ye said, O house of Israel: for I know the things that come into your mind, every one of them.*

Jeremiah 30:2

Thus speaketh the LORD God of Israel, saying, Write thee all the words that I have spoken unto thee in a book.

CHAPTER 20: THE MEN OF HAMPTON COURT NOT INSPIRED

Jeremiah 36:1, 2

> *And it came to pass in the fourth year of Jehoiakim the son of Josiah king of Judah, that this word came unto Jeremiah from the LORD, saying, Take thee a roll of a book, and write therein all the words that I have spoken unto thee against Israel, and against Judah, and against all the nations, from the day I spake unto thee, from the days of Josiah, even unto this day.*

As you can see, it mentions over and over again that God revealed His word by speaking, by the words of His mouth and even telling them to write it in a book. The phrase "The word of the Lord came..." 92 times with 47 of those being in the book of Ezekiel. The phrase "Thus saith the Lord..." is in the Bible 413 times.

Were the Translators of the Kings James Bible inspired? Were they given the words of the Word of God by God?

There are those who teach that they were including Peter Ruckman, Gail Riplinger and now a man with the initials D.B. He (D.B.) said,

> "The King James Bible is inspired because All Scripture is given by inspiration, and if the Holy Spirit guided the translators to choose the right words, then the King James Bible is inspired."

He told me that he did not believe in dual inspiration but that is exactly what this is. Then he also told me in a computer conversation,

> "There was no perfect Bible until the King James Bible."

Let me tell you what others *correctly* teach about whether the translators were inspired.

Dr. Sorenson –

> "There is absolutely no record or claim that the King James Bible translators as godly as they were, received any such inspiration. A careful study of their work and the subsequent publishing process absolutely militates against any such notion. The King James Bible as a translation is not inspired."

Dr. Brown –

> ""God inspired His words only when they flowed from the tip of the pens of the various Scriptural authors. He has not done so again. I do not believe in double inspiration of any type no matter who promotes it. While God has not re-inspired the King James Bible, 'I believe that the King James Bible is God's word kept intact in English' (quoting Dr. Sorenson) The King James Bible translators had God's preserved words in front of them as they worked with the Hebrew Masoretic text and the Greek Traditional text! They did not need to be re-inspired, they simply needed to faithfully and accurately translate those preserved words and that is what they did! That outcome is that the King James Bible is God's Word kept intact in English."

Dr. Stringer –

> "I do not believe that the King James Bible is inspired. Inspiration happened only once; that is when God took control of a person and spoke His words through them or caused them to write down His words. That is not because I believe that there is any weakness or any inferiority in the Kings James Bible. I believe the Kings James Bible is perfect and inerrant! There is nothing about the

CHAPTER 20: THE MEN OF HAMPTON COURT NOT INSPIRED

King James Bible that needs to be corrected or improved. But, God inspired His words only once, when they flowed from the tip of the pens of the various Scriptural writers. He has not done it again! The Words of God have been settled in heaven. God gave some of them to Moses to record on earth. He gave some to Jeremiah, some to Paul, some to Peter and so on. They recorded the exact words that God gave them. God finished delivering His words to men as John finished the Book of Revelation. That is how inspiration works."

Dr. Mann –

"If by the phrase 'the King James Bible is inspired' you mean that the men who translated the Word of God from the Hebrew, Aramaic and Greek to the English were inspired, I do not believe that. The inspiration took place to the Holy men of God who were moved by the Holy Spirit and that inspiration ended with the last word of the last sentence of the Book of Revelation in the originals. They have been preserved since then. The translators never claimed inspiration and nowhere in the Scriptures does God attribute that to them. If by the phrase the King James Bible is inspired you mean that the infallible, inerrant and preserved Word of God is there in its entirety by faithful and accurate translation, then that is what I believe. The King James Bible is the preserved Word of God."

I describe dual or double inspiration this way. "Inspiration happened in the Hebrew, Aramaic and Greek between Genesis and Revelation. When God finished telling John the last word of the last sentence of the last verse in the last book Revelation, inspiration ceased. What would be dual inspiration is if God or the Holy Spirit told or guided the translators to write or choose the correct words in English." – Gary Mann

Look again at the included 15 rules the translators went by in their work of translation and the letter from the translators to the readers and to King James.

RICHARD BANCROFT'S RULES TO BE OBSERVED IN THE TRANSLATION OF THE BIBLE.

1. The ordinary Bible read in the church, commonly called the Bishops' Bible, to be followed, and as little altered as the truth of the original will permit.

2. The names of the prophets, and the holy writers, with the other names in the text, to be retained as near as may be, accordingly as they are vulgarly used.

3. The old ecclesiastical words to be kept, namely, as the word church not to be translated congregation &c.

4. When any word hath divers significations, that to be kept which hath been most commonly used by the most eminent Fathers, being agreeable to the propriety of the place, and the analogy of faith.

CHAPTER 20: THE MEN OF HAMPTON COURT NOT INSPIRED

5. The division of the chapters to be altered either not at all, or as little as may be, if necessity so require.

6. No marginal notes at all to be affixed, but only for the explanation of the Hebrew or Greek words, which cannot without some circumlocution so briefly and fitly be expressed in the text.

7. Such quotations of places to be marginally set down, as shall serve for the fit reference of one Scripture to another.

8. Every particular man of each company to take the same chapter or chapters; and having translated or amended them severally by himself, where he thinks good, all to meet together, confer what they have done, and agree for their part what shall stand.

9. As any one company hath dispatched any one book in this manner, they shall send it to the rest, to be considered of seriously and judiciously; for his Majesty is very careful in this point.

10. If any company, upon the review of the book so sent, shall doubt or differ upon any places, to send them word thereof, note the places, and therewithal send their reasons; to which if they consent not, the difference to be compounded at the general meeting, which is to be of the chief persons of each company, at the end of the work.

11. When any place of special obscurity is doubted of, letters to be directed by authority, to send to any learned man in the land for his judgment in such a place.

12. Letters to be sent from every Bishop to the rest of his clergy, admonishing them of this Translation in hand; and to move and charge as many as, being skilful in the tongues, have taken pains in that kind, to send his particular observations to the company, either at Westminster, Cambridge, or Oxford.

13. The directors in each company to be the Deans of Westminster and Chester, for that place; and the King's Professors in the Hebrew and Greek in either University.

14. These translations to be used, when they agree better with the text than the Bishops' Bible: Tyndale's, Matthew's, Coverdale's, Whitchurch's [Great], Geneva.

15. Besides the said directions before mentioned, three or four of the most ancient and grave divines in either of the Universities, not employed in translating, to be assigned by the Vice-Chancellor, upon conference with the rest of the Heads, to be overseers of the Translations, as well Hebrew as Greek, for the better observation of the fourth rule above specified.

CHAPTER 20: THE MEN OF HAMPTON COURT NOT INSPIRED

Other Reasons Why the King James Bible Translators were not inspired.

Questions…If the men of Hampton Court were inspired…

1. Why did it take them 7 years (1604-1611) to complete the work?
2. Why 6 different companies to translate and compare their work among themselves? (#8-10)
3. Why compare their work to previous translations? (#1, 14)
4. Why did they consult with other people outside their company? (#11, 12)
5. Why didn't they say they were inspired like the Prophets and Apostles did?
6. Why did they say they revised their work? (Opening statement – "Translated out of the original tongues and with the former translations diligently compared and revised by His Majesty's special command.")

They indicated it took much time to do the work of translation.

They understood the process of inspiration, preservation and translation.

They knew what translation work involved.

They said they translated out of the original tongues. (See opening statement in vi. above)

Conclusion, we have the verbal and plenary inspired Word of God by preservation and faithful and accurate translation in the King James Bible keeping all the infallibility, inerrancy and authority of what God originally inspired.

No, the translators were not inspired! They faithfully, carefully and meticulously translated the Bible from the original languages into the receptor language, English. From the process of Inspiration, Preservation and Translation we have the verbally inspired and perfectly preserved Word of God in the English language in the King James Bible and need no other English translation. What Marvel!

1 Peter 1:25

> *"But the word of the Lord endureth for ever. And this is the word which by the gospel is preached unto you."*

ABOUT THE AUTHOR

I was born in 1950 and born again in 1973. I began preaching and being a personal soul winner in 1975 not knowing what the Lord had for me to do but now after 45 plus years of preaching and winning people to Christ I have been used both nationally and in some foreign countries. All the glory goes to our Lord and Saviour Jesus Christ in it all. I have been used to start a church in Delaware, Ohio from 1982 until 1995. In 1995 I resigned as Pastor and started my work as an Evangelist.

My wife and I were married in 1973 and now have 3 daughters who are all serving the Lord with their husbands and families in different parts of America. They have blessed us with 11 grandchildren all of whom have been saved.

I have a Bachelor's degree in Pastoral Theology, a Master's degree, an honorary Doctor of Divinity, and though I am finished with my college years I am ever striving to learn and pass on to the next generation and beyond all I have learned. My personal motto is based on 2 Timothy 2:15 which says, *"Study to shew thyself approved unto God, a workman that needeth not to be ashamed, rightly dividing the word of truth."* My motto is: "If study causes us to rightly divide the truth, a lack of study will cause us to wrongly divide it."

www.ingramcontent.com/pod-product-compliance
Lightning Source LLC
Chambersburg PA
CBHW051047160426
43193CB00010B/1100